HAND IN HAND

Growing Spiritually With Our Children

by Sue Downing

DISCIPLESHIP RESOURCES

P.O. BOX 840 • NASHVILLE, TENNESSEE 37202-0840

ISBN 0-88177-224-0

Library of Congress Catalog Card No. 97-66521

Cover illustration: ©1998 by Roseanne Spiess Giles

DR224

Presented to

_____

by

_____

on

_____

Table of Contents

Introduction

Lord,

We come before you in prayer for our children.

Help us to lovingly reach out, clasp their hands, and draw them ever nearer to you.

Make us aware of the tremendous privilege and responsibility we are entrusted with.

Guide us as we try to nurture our children's understanding of what it means to pray.

Give us the ability to explore the Bible with our children so that they may come to know you and your will for their lives.

Instill within us ways to show our children an appreciation for your world.

Awaken in us the need to become an active part of the community of faith.

Impress on our hearts the importance of celebrating and sharing special times together in the life of the church.

Fill us with your love so that we are able to embrace our children during times of sadness, confusion, and doubt.

Help us to feel our children's trusting hands holding ours.

Help us as, hand in hand, we grow in faith together!

Amen

Preface

I have written this book as an expression of thanks from my heart to my parents and the countless others in the faith community who helped instill within me the foundation for a growing Christian faith. This loving process had its beginnings when my parents chose to have me baptized into Christ's holy church. At that time, they and the entire church family promised to nurture me in the Christian faith and acknowledged what God's grace had already accomplished. In making this decision, my parents gave me the most precious gift I could ever receive—a gift that, through God's infinite love, has blessed and sustained me; a gift that touches not only my life but the lives of many; a gift that will continue to give and grow in meaning forever.

The book *Hand in Hand* extends a very special invitation to you. It invites you to come, listen, and obey Jesus' words, "Let the little children come to me; do not stop them; for it is to such as these that the kingdom of God belongs" (Mark 10:14b). It invites you to come and commit yourselves to the tremendous privilege and responsibility of sharing the Christian faith with your children. It invites you to come and discover ways to grow with your children spiritually. It invites you to come and give your children the greatest gift you can!

1

Praying With Our Children

It was a special time in the life of our family. Julie, our eighteen-year-old daughter, was about to begin her freshman year at Furman University in Greenville, South Carolina, about four hundred miles from our Nashville home. Along with some feelings of apprehension, Julie was truly excited about her new adventure. As her dad and I helped Julie prepare to leave, it seems we spent a great deal of time that summer determining what things she would need, making lists of items, gathering the items, and finally packing everything. These "necessities" eventually filled up every available space in our car plus a U-Haul trailer.

As we went through this process of preparation together, my thoughts frequently carried me back to Julie's childhood, a time her dad and I can now reclaim only with our memories, a time that seems like just yesterday. As I remembered, the realization came to me again that childhood is when we as parents can help instill in our children the priceless gift of a growing faith in God. This is when we have the tremendous privilege and responsibility to begin to pack the real necessities for Christian living within our children's hearts. But unlike the confines of the cars and trailers in our material world, our children's hearts always have room for more growth; and the usefulness of what we give to our children goes on forever!

How, then, do we go about the task of equipping our children to live the Christian life? What necessities do our children need? This book began with a prayer. That is where we will begin, for prayer is at the very foundation for a growing faith in God. Prayer is our personal link with God. Through prayer we can come to know God as our constant friend and

Lord, we come before you in prayer for our children.

Help us to lovingly reach out, clasp their hands, and draw them ever nearer to you.

Guide us as we try to nurture our children's understanding of what it means to pray.

companion. When we teach our children the importance of prayer in their lives, we give them the "blessed assurance" that God is always with them. They are never alone.

Wouldn't it be wonderful if we could jump into our cars, go to the nearest mall, purchase the gift of prayer, and wrap it with brightly colored paper to give to our children at an early age? While on the surface this might sound great, deep within us we know that our most cherished gifts are the ones that come from the heart and are wrapped securely with love.

Most of us have no doubt that we want prayer to become an integral part of our children's lives. The desire is there, but sometimes so is the hesitancy. There are many reasons for this. As with so many things, some of us simply do not know when or how to begin teaching our children about prayer. Others feel that they do not know enough about prayer. Still others have not grown up in a home centered around prayer and feel uncomfortable with it. Then there are those who feel that the church has the sole responsibility to teach our children about prayer. Basically, a sense of inadequacy underlies each of these reasons.

The purpose of this chapter is to ease these fears and look together at a workable guide for helping instill in our children the practice of prayer. Let us first look at how and when we begin. Through prayer we have the ability to embrace our children with God's love. When we pray for our children and God's guidance in leading our children, we accomplish two things: We place our children in God's hands, and we give ourselves the inner assurance that we are not alone in our endeavors. God is with us each step of the way. When we go to God daily in prayer for our children, we are giving them a priceless gift of far more worth than any material thing imaginable. Through prayer we can ask that God's presence be in our children's lives, that they be guided by the Holy Spirit, and that they experience God's love and forgiveness. We can pray that they make the right choices and come to realize their God-given gifts. We can pray that we as parents are forever faithful in praying for our children. No matter where we are in our prayer lives, as we commit to taking that initial step in prayer for our children, we discover that we will grow and be blessed in our prayer lives, too. We will also find that our children have much to teach us about prayer.

When do we begin? We begin this moment, this day. We begin as our children are born, lifting up prayers of praise and thanksgiving for them, and remembering that children are a gift from the Lord and a real blessing. We begin as early as we can, recognizing that the most important thing is that we do begin!

When children are infants, we have the opportunity to experience prayer with them in unique ways. Let me suggest the following:

- Music is a beautiful means of prayer. Spend precious time with your baby by singing or playing songs of prayer, hymns, and soothing lullabies. Some of my fondest memories are of singing "Jesus Loves Me," "What a Friend We Have in Jesus," and countless other songs to Julie.
- Loving actions are prayers. When we hold our babies close, rock them, care for their needs, simply take time to interact with them, we give thanks to God for the gift of our children and show them that they are loved.
- Pray silently, verbally, in whatever manner you feel comfortable, for the gift of new life you have been entrusted with. Pray for yourselves as parents.
- Invite older siblings to sing and say prayers with you for a new baby in the family. Then express your thanks for each family member.

The sacrament of baptism is in itself an act of prayer, through which we recognize that our children belong to God and we commit with the entire congregation to nurture them in the Christian faith.

As children become toddler age and older, many more moments for helping them understand prayer present themselves. There is one type of opportunity that transcends all the rest, and you will hear it mentioned many times throughout this book: The best teaching tool we have as parents is our example. Children of any age are keen observers, and little eyes and ears are often watching and listening when we are completely unaware of it. When children see us praying,

When we go to God daily in prayer for our children, we are giving them a priceless gift of far more worth than any material thing imaginable.

good things can result. Parents who pray regularly impress upon their children the importance of prayer. Children come to realize that prayer is not limited to any particular age group. We give them a tangible model to go by as they observe when, why, and how we pray. We are planting the seeds for future families to engage in prayer.

Besides role modeling prayer for our children, we need to be intentional about seeking ways to pray with them and helping them discover the beauty of prayer. In both instances we first need a clear image in our minds of the nature of prayer.

Prayer is both talking and listening to God. We can choose to pray to God anywhere, anytime, no matter what we have done or how we feel. There is no rigid set of rules for how to pray. We can sing, shout, whisper, or think our prayers. We can fold our hands, kneel with heads bowed, stand, or dance. However we pray, we can know in our hearts that God is always ready to listen to and love us just as we are. Prayer gives us the inner assurance that we are never alone. We have a constant friend we can talk to!

Ironically, it is often our children who teach us this. My mother-in-law tells how my husband, Jim, said his bedtime prayers as a little boy. He went through a long list of thank-you's and then closed his prayer by saying, "G'bye, 'Dod,' see you tomorrow!" He was genuinely talking with God as he would his best friend. He was "telling it like it is."

Our children's attitude toward prayer is also shaped by the messages we give them about *why* we pray. I believe that the universal question for children is, Why? Why we pray is at the heart of building a strong prayer relationship with God. Again, as we look at ways to make prayer a vital part of family life, I think it is most helpful to picture God as the most extraordinary friend we have ever had. That is why we lift our prayers to God to praise and thank God; to ask God's forgiveness for others and for ourselves; and, finally, to take time to listen to God.

With all these thoughts in mind, let us visualize more ways to touch our children's lives with prayer.

BECOME ATTUNED TO SPONTANEOUS MOMENTS FOR PRAYER

These unplanned moments of opportunity can be some of the most rewarding times we spend with children. They appear through varied situations at any age, time, and place, and can be wonderful stepping stones for prayer, conversations about God, and loving actions for God. Like so many things, though, once we let these opportune moments escape us, we may never recapture them again. How, then, do we recognize these moments?

- Unexpected times of joy and celebration—a family picnic, a surprise visit by someone, a homemade gift received from your child—invite a simple one- or two-sentence prayer of praise and thanksgiving.

- The wonders of nature and the changing of the seasons offer endless moments of serendipity! Twinkling stars at night, a rainbow, winter's first snowfall, a fuzzy caterpillar, a field of daisies—all are invitations to pray with your child.

- Moments of closeness with children can prompt us to pray. A story shared, your child's hug, "I love you," outstretched arms, a hand-picked bouquet of dandelions just for you, can touch our hearts and turn our thoughts toward God.

WEAVE INTENTIONAL PRAYER EXPERIENCES WITHIN FAMILY LIFE

Regular prayer within everyday life teaches children that we need to set aside daily times to pray. It lays the groundwork for a consistent pattern of prayer. Mealtimes and bedtime immediately come to mind. It is easy for prayers at these times to evolve into rote repetition of the same words over and over again. While repeated prayers have their purpose, you can help make your child's prayer experience more meaningful by asking your child to add his or her own words to the prayer, by reading or having your child read a different prayer occasionally, or by selecting a prayer such as the Doxology to sing together.

I like what Jo Carr had to say about prayer at mealtime in her book *Touch the Wind: Creative Worship With Children*: "Give thanks at mealtime. Simply. Honestly. Avoid ecclesias-

> There is no rigid set of rules for how to pray. We can sing, shout, whisper, or think our prayers.

tical jargon, but thank God instead for the good-smelling stew. And receive graciously the *child's* prayer of thanks for ketchup. It is a valid and lovely prayer" (Copyright © 1975 by Discipleship Resources—The Upper Room; All rights reserved; Used by permission of the publisher; pages 62–63).

Bedtime is another time to set aside daily for prayer. Unlike table grace, bedtime prayers are an exceptional opportunity to encourage children to pray about their day, people in their lives, or whatever they want to talk to God about.

Listen with your heart as well as your mind to what your children are praying. Prayers can be revealing and can give you insight into a child's feelings about God, themselves, others, and situations at home, school, or other places.

When our daughter was very young, I began sitting with her at bedtime to listen to her prayers, pray with her, and sing to her. These moments opened the door for Julie and me to communicate with each other about all sorts of things, and I would not have exchanged them for anything!

HELP YOUR CHILDREN EXPRESS THEIR PRAYERS IN A VARIETY OF WAYS

Speaking

Young children can begin praying by saying simple one- or two-sentence prayers of praise and thanks, such as, "I love you, God. Thank you for my mommy and daddy." As children grow older, they can be encouraged to expand the length of their spoken prayers and to pray verbally in front of others, such as at family gatherings.

Art

Children about four years old and older can express prayers through art. They can create picture prayers using crayons, paint, chalk, or cut-out pictures. The pictures can show God what they are thankful for, or people or situations they are concerned about. Or the pictures can simply be the children's own gift to God.

Writing

Older children can begin to write their prayers down. Your child could keep these prayers in a booklet or could write a prayer to give to someone.

Actions

Help your children realize that we pray to God through our bodies as well as through our words. For younger children, folding their hands, kneeling, and bowing their heads can represent prayer. Prayer time is an excellent time for you and your child to learn some simple sign language. A number of books provide instruction in sign language. Begin by learning to sign together the prayer, "I love you, God." Then increase your child's signing vocabulary as he or she matures. Older children can also understand that anytime they reach out in love to others, they are expressing their love to God.

Music

Music—not only singing but also playing an instrument— can be a beautiful way for a family to pray together. Through music we can also familiarize our children with many of the traditional hymns.

Thought

Children can grow in the understanding that we pray to God through our thoughts. We can help them understand that they can think their prayers at any time and in what-ever place they may be. This particular expression of prayer reinforces the idea that God is always with them. When you pray with your children in this manner, hold them close or hold their hands.

GRADUALLY INTRODUCE ALL THE COMPONENTS OF PRAYER

The components of prayer include giving praise and thanks, asking for forgiveness (confession), praying for ourselves (petition) and for others (intercession), and listening to God. Very young children can begin with prayers of praise and thanks to God. As children become older, help them pray for

Listen with your heart as well as your mind to what your children are praying.

the needs of others. Emphasize to children that this is a way of showing our love to others.

Be sensitive to incidents that children have remorse about. Encourage them to express their feelings to God. Say to them: "God sometimes does not like what we do, but God never stops loving us, and God listens when we say we are sorry."

In teaching children about praying for themselves, de-emphasize praying for material things. Stress asking for God's help in their relationships with others, asking for guidance as to specific actions they can take to help God, and just expressing to God what is on their minds.

A vital part of prayer is listening to God. This concept is difficult even for adults to grasp. Our overall tendency is to think of prayer as talking, not as listening. Younger children can learn to "be still" and listen to God through the sounds of God's world—the singing of birds, the tapping of rain on our windows, the rustling of leaves in the trees. Older children can start to comprehend that God "speaks" to them through others—through a hug, a smile, a kind deed. They can also be led to listen for feelings that God gives them, such as love for others, forgiveness, thankfulness, or a willingness to do something. As children grow into adulthood, their view of what it means to listen to God can significantly shape their response to God's call and their use of their God-given gifts.

Listening to God also encompasses listening for answers to our prayers. In this area it is important that we help our children come to certain realizations:

- God is faithful to answer all our prayers. Sometimes God responds to our prayers in ways we do not understand or expect, but we can trust that God loves us.

- There are instances when it takes a long time for God to answer our prayers. This is not because God is too busy for us or wants us to cease praying about something.

- God is not like Santa Claus or a catalog that we can order things from. The one constant that we can always anticipate from God is God's love.

- It pleases God when we give our thanks for answered prayer.

Children are best led to these realizations by their parents' example. Let your children hear you pray, or say a prayer of thanks with them for answered prayer. Allow children to observe you in prayer and listen to what you pray for. Parents who pray for a new car should not be surprised if their child prays for a bicycle. Tell your children how God has answered your prayer requests, especially in instances in which you have prayed for a long time about a particular situation.

I had prayed since Julie was ten years old that a family misunderstanding would be resolved. She was aware of my prayers. Ten years later, when Julie was twenty years old, healing occurred and a beautiful reunion took place within our family. What a blessed time it was as we thanked and praised God for it together. Show your children trust, patience, and a thankful heart in your prayer life, and you will teach them these attitudes.

PRAY THE LORD'S PRAYER

The Lord's Prayer, found in Matthew 6:9b-13, is an important prayer that people of all ages, including our children, need to be exposed to. Jesus prayed this prayer to God, his heavenly Father. Through the Lord's Prayer, Jesus helps us to better understand the nature of prayer. Jesus shows us how we need to pray and what we need to pray about. Let us look at this prayer together.

> Our Father in heaven,
>   hallowed be your name.
>   Your kingdom come.
>   Your will be done,
>   on earth as it is in heaven.
>   Give us this day our daily bread.
>   And forgive us our debts,
>   as we also have forgiven our debtors.
>   And do not bring us to the time of trial,
>   but rescue us from the evil one.

In teaching our children about the Lord's Prayer, we need to begin by telling them that this is an important prayer that comes from Jesus. Say: "This prayer is found in the Bible. We pray the Lord's Prayer during worship at church, in Sunday school, and at many other times, too." Take time to sit with your child, find the Lord's Prayer in the Bible, and let

Allow children to observe you in prayer and listen to what you pray for.

your young child hold the Bible as you read the prayer. Older children could be encouraged to read the prayer with you. Then look at the prayer again together, a phrase at a time, exploring the words and their meaning. As children read the prayer from the Bible, they may notice that the phrase "For thine is the kingdom and the power and the glory, forever. Amen," which they say in church, is not in the Bible. Explain that this phrase was added by the church as a closing to the prayer. Help children understand the meaning of the prayer by using simple words that are a part of their vocabulary. For example, a six- to seven-year-old would better understand the Lord's Prayer through these words:

God, I am so glad that I belong to you and
    you care about me.
Thank you for loving me and being my
    friend who is always with me.
Help everyone to be kind to one another and
    to know that you love them.
Thank you for our world and for giving us
    what we need.
We are sorry when we do things that make
    you sad.
Show us how to be more loving and the
    many ways we can help you.
I love you very much, God!
Amen.

When you take time to talk with your children, don't do all the talking yourself. Invite them to express their feelings about what the Lord's Prayer means. Give them the opportunity to ask questions. If you do not have an answer to a question, be honest and tell them so. Go to your pastor, the church library, or another reliable source to seek out an answer. Realize that teaching children about the Lord's Prayer is an ongoing process. As an adult, I continue to glean new meaning from this prayer depending upon what I am experiencing and where I am in my faith walk. Be open to discussing the Lord's Prayer with your children over and over! In so doing, you will grow in your understanding of it as they grow in theirs. Above all, remember to ask God's guidance before each encounter. Pray that God gives you the thoughts, words, and actions to help instill in your children what they need to know.

WHEN WE PRAY WITH OUR CHILDREN,

- we pray for and with our children, seeking God's guidance in all we do;

- we learn to become attuned to spontaneous moments for prayer;

- we weave intentional prayer experiences within our family life;

- we help our children express their prayers in a variety of ways;

- we listen with our hearts as well as with our minds to what our children are praying;

- we gradually introduce all the components of prayer to our children;

- we look to the Bible, and specifically to the Lord's Prayer, as a wonderful source for instructing our children.

READING THE BIBLE WITH OUR CHILDREN

Lord, we come before you in prayer for our children.

Help us to lovingly reach out, clasp their hands, and draw them ever nearer to you.

Give us the ability to explore the Bible with our children so that they may come to know you and your will for their lives.

One of my favorite hymns is "Jesus Loves Me," by Anna B. Warner. I listened to and sang this song as a child. I sang it as a mother to my daughter, Julie. I sing it with the children I teach. A close friend sang it at our son's memorial service. The words are lovingly etched in my mind and will forever have a cherished place in my heart. Its message is ageless and timeless:

> Jesus loves me! This I know,
> for the Bible tells me so.
> Little ones to him belong;
> they are weak, but he is strong.
> Yes, Jesus loves me!
> Yes, Jesus loves me!
> Yes, Jesus loves me!
> The Bible tells me so.

Often this familiar hymn is one of the first songs, if not *the* first song, that children learn in Sunday school. The words tell them how they are loved by Jesus, and also about an important book called the Bible.

The Bible is frequently called the greatest book ever written. It provides the basis for our faith. The Bible is the Word of God. Within its pages are the story of God's love for us, and guidance on how God's children are to live. It is a book that helps us to personally know God and Jesus. It is a book we never stop learning or growing from. How desperately we need to share it and explore it with our children!

Just as with prayer, the majority of parents do not need convincing that their children need to be exposed to the Bible.

What often hinders that exposure are those recurring feelings of inadequacy. As a result, there is a tendency to leave "Bible training" to the church. On the contrary, while church is certainly a valid place for our children to learn about the Bible, the church cannot realistically be expected to bear all the responsibility. Optimum learning takes place when home and church work together as a team.

How do we as parents strive to accomplish this? How do we fulfill our portion of the partnership? Let me suggest that it helps us greatly as parents to view our role with our children as learners as well as teachers. When we do this, we give ourselves a whole new perspective on exposing our children to the Bible. I have led an adult Bible study group for the past four years. I agreed to do this, not because I consider myself a biblical scholar, but because I felt a real need and desire to continue to learn more about the Bible. I knew that through the preparation and study needed to lead my Bible study group, I would also receive the gift of learning and would be immensely blessed in my endeavors. This has proven true over and over again throughout my life. If parents wait until they feel that they have gained "enough" biblical knowledge to guide their children, there will never be a starting point; for not one of us ever ceases the need to grow in our understanding of the Word of God.

When we attempt to bring the Bible to life for our children, we must also remember that God is right here at our side to direct and sustain us. This assurance has given me the confidence and ability to commit to teach my own child about God, to be a children's Sunday school teacher, to write children's Sunday school curriculum, and to do countless other things that I felt God's call to do. So as we step out in faith for our children, we know that we are not alone and that we can become active participants with our children. Parents and children are learning and growing spiritually together!

Once parents make the loving commitment to trust in God's leading and explore the Bible with their children, they are faced with the question, How can we most effectively accomplish this? The awareness that the Bible is meant to be a hands-on book is a primary key to the answer of this question. As children's coordinator for our church a number of years ago, I was asked to present a message to our third graders, who were receiving their own Bibles as a gift from the church. As a part of my message I compared the Bible to a pair of blue jeans. I explained that when we get a brand-new pair of jeans and put them on for the first time, they feel stiff and uncomfortable. If we leave the jeans hanging unused in a closet, the jeans will be nice to look at but will remain stiff and uncomfortable. Only when we consistently wear and wash our jeans—in other words, use them—do they gradually become soft and comfortable. The Bible is not a book meant to sit on a shelf for visual purposes. It is a book to be held, read, taken to church, taught from, and lived. Only then is it transformed into something familiar and comfortable for us. A pastor I once worked with always presented the children in the church with red Bibles. As he gave these to the children, he said, "The color red is a reminder that the Bible needs to be read!" Let us now identify some specific ways for the Bible to be a hands-on book within our families.

GIVE YOUR CHILD HIS OR HER OWN BIBLE

While a child traditionally receives a Bible from the church around third grade, children can also benefit from receiving a Bible before that time. Dismiss the feeling that it is a wasted effort to give children more than one Bible. I still treasure the Bible my grandparents gave to me on my fifth birthday. Even though I could not read it or have a deep understanding of all the words at that time, I could know that it was a special book that was given to me out of love. I could take it to church with me just like my parents did. As I grew older, I could read it and grow spiritually from its message. Many years and Bibles later, I could still hold that Bible and be forever thankful that it was given to me. When we give the gift of a Bible to our children, we help impart to them that this book is important in our lives as well as in theirs. When we place a Bible in our children's hands, we are planting the seeds for their spiritual growth.

It is important to note here that all Bibles are not alike and that some versions are more appropriate for children than others. In addition to Bibles, there are also Bible storybooks that tell and illustrate selected Bible stories. Often the first

If parents wait until they feel that they have gained "enough" biblical knowledge to guide their children, there will never be a starting point; for not one of us ever ceases the need to grow in our understanding of the Word of God.

"Bible" a young child receives is a Bible storybook. Just as with most other things, parents need to go beyond the overall look of a Bible or a Bible storybook to select the best one for their children. Here are some guidelines to help you:

- Ask your pastor or other church staff to recommend a Bible or Bible storybook that would be suitable for your child.

- Always take the time to carefully examine a Bible or Bible storybook before purchasing one. Ask yourself, "Is this on a level my child would understand? What supplementary resources—such as maps, a dictionary, and pictures—are included?" If the Bible contains questions for you to discuss with your child, make sure they are not posed in such a way that would frighten your child or that presents views contrary to your beliefs.

- While looks should not be the single criteria for the selection of a Bible, it is good to find one that you feel would be visually attractive to your child, as well as one that appears sturdy. You are giving your child a Bible to be used and carried with him or her, not to stay on a shelf.

- Recognize that as your children grow, so will their need for different types of Bibles and Bible storybooks. The Bible storybook you purchased for a four-year-old child would most likely not be suitable for an eight-year-old.

- If circumstances allow, plan an outing with your child to purchase a Bible for him or her. Do this only after looking at Bibles yourself and having one or more in mind that would be appropriate for your child. When you arrive home, place your child's name in the Bible, or let your child write his or her name. This helps to give children a feeling of real ownership for their Bibles.

SET AN EXAMPLE FOR YOUR CHILDREN

If we wish for the Bible to play a vital role in our children's lives, we must show them that it plays a vital role in ours. Telling without actually doing leaves only a surface impression. Let your child observe you reading and studying the Bible on a daily basis. Be intentional about carrying the Bible to church with you and following the Scripture lesson in your own Bible as it is read in the worship service. Agree to host a Bible study, or several sessions of one, in your home. Make the commitment to purposely schedule family devotionals that include, among other things, prayer and sharing and reading from the Bible. Plan for your family to participate together in devotional times during vacations as well. This speaks to our children that wherever we are and whatever we are doing, we should always include moments for God.

A primary part of setting an example is becoming involved. Actively seek and join a Sunday school class centered around the Bible. Commit to join a Bible study offered through the church. The DISCIPLE Bible study series (Nashville: The United Methodist Publishing House) presents a wonderful opportunity to do this. Agree to teach your child's Sunday school class, vacation Bible school, or another program focused on Bible study. Any involvement of this kind serves a twofold purpose: first, you are increasing your knowledge of the Bible; and second, your children are being made aware that you are studying, learning, and teaching about the Bible.

When our daughter was a young child, I had my devotion, or "quiet time," in the early morning; and I always had it in the same place. These moments centered around prayer and reading the Bible. I did not realize the impact this had on Julie until years later when Julie, then a college student, told me about the positive impression it had made on her. Now, as a young woman she has identified her time and place to commune with God through prayer and reading the Bible. Along the same lines, Julie has observed her father over the years diligently studying Scripture to lead an adult Sunday school class. What valuable lessons we teach through our example!

TALK WITH YOUR CHILDREN ABOUT THE BIBLE

Children can be introduced to the Bible at an early age. Your toddler and preschooler can look through its pages and know that this is a special book that tells about Jesus, God, and God's love for them. As parents we can read and talk with our children about stories from the Bible. I teach three- and four-year-olds at our church's day school. Recently I asked my group of children individually what their favorite bedtime stories were. How encouraging it was when little Zachary replied without hesitation, "My Bible storybook!"

If we wish for the Bible to play a vital role in our children's lives, we must show them that it plays a vital role in ours.

Reading the Bible With Our Children

Read Bible stories frequently to your children at bedtime, family devotional times, or other designated times. First review any story you read to make sure the wording and pictures are not presented in a way that frightens your child. Children need to see the Bible as a book of love, not of fear. Discover with your children where a particular story is located in the Bible. Let your children hold the open Bible as you read the story with them, or invite them to hold the open Bible as their contribution to a family devotional. When you have finished reading a Bible story together, ask your children to repeat the story back to you in their own words. If you wish, write down what they say and help them create their own Bible storybook. They could be encouraged to illustrate their stories. In addition to reading stories together, you can look up verses that your children have learned in Sunday school, say the verses together, and talk about their meaning.

SING AND PLAY

Young children are fascinated with pretending as they play, and they love action rhymes. Often Sunday school literature has Bible story rhymes with suggested motions. Look for these in the leaflets your child brings home from Sunday school. Make up rhymes and actions yourself by reading a story from the Sunday school curriculum and asking yourself, "What action can I pair with these words?" Have fun doing these rhymes with your children. Here is an example of one:

JESUS TEACHES US TO PRAY
The disciples talked with Jesus one day. (*Move fingers of both hands in an open/shut motion.*)
Please Lord, teach us (*Point to self.*)
how to pray. (*Fold hands in prayer.*)
Jesus showed his loving care, (*Cross hands over heart.*)
by praying with them a special prayer. (*Fold hands in prayer.*)
Jesus also gives (*Extend arms outward.*)
this prayer (*Fold hands in prayer.*)
for me and you. (*Point to self and others.*)
For we can learn from Jesus too! (*Extend outstretched arms upward.*)

(From *Come Follow Jesus, Vacation Bible School 1996, Ages 5–6 Teacher,* written by Sue Downing, copyright © 1995 Cokesbury; page 24.)

Children of all ages love and learn from songs. Songs are a wonderful means for introducing your children to the Bible. Keep abreast especially of songs sung in Sunday school, vacation Bible school, children's choir, and other such programs. Sing these songs frequently with your children as part of a family devotional time, or while taking a walk together, riding in the car, or just being together.

STUDY TOGETHER

Older children learn that the Bible consists of many books and that these books make up two parts of the Bible, called the Old Testament and the New Testament. As you continue to set aside moments for Bible study with your children, examine together which book and testament the passage you are reading is found in. Gradually work together toward your children being able to look up Scripture themselves and read simple verses to you. Explain to your children that all the books of the Bible teach us about God and God's people, but that the stories in the New Testament help us know God's Son, Jesus. Lead your children to begin to understand that while the Bible was written a long time ago by many different people and is about people who lived in a different age, it is God's extraordinary way of speaking to us today and always. Say: "Through the Bible we can know about God, Jesus, God's love for us, and how God wants us to live."

As your children mature, you will have the opportunity to foster new ways for them to explore the Bible. Look at a Bible concordance and atlas together. Invite your children to take a more active role in family devotional times by selecting and reading a Scripture verse or story, or by simply telling something new they have learned about the Bible. Encourage them to have a personal daily devotion time during which they read from their Bibles and spend time in prayer. Suggestions for structured, individual readings can be obtained from Sunday school curriculum, your church staff, or children's devotional materials such as *Pockets*, a great resource published by The Upper Room. Information about *Pockets* and other resources recommended in this book can be found in the "Suggested Resources" list beginning on page 86.

Read Bible stories frequently to your children at bedtime, family devotional times, or other designated times.

Reading the Bible With Our Children

A PLACE TO START

Listed below are some important Bible passages that you will want your children to become familiar with. Since children continue to grow in their understanding of the Bible as they mature, Bible stories need to be told over and over again. For example, a ten-year-old, who has experienced the joys and challenges of navigating several years of school, will understand the Twenty-third Psalm in ways that are different from a three-year-old, who is still very dependent upon parents. When your child is very young, you will want to focus upon those stories and verses that reinforce the loving and caring nature of God. As children become a little older, they can be introduced to a wider range of Bible stories. As the stories of the Bible become part of the fabric of your children's lives, your children will be able to draw strength, courage, and wisdom from the stories as they continue to grow in faith.

• Creation—Genesis 1–2

• God's covenant with Noah—Genesis 6:9–9:17

• Abraham and Sarah—Genesis 17:1–18:15; 21:1-6

• Isaac and Rebekah—Genesis 24

• Esau and Jacob—Genesis 25:27-34, 27:1–28:5

• Joseph and his brothers—Genesis 37:1-28; 39:1–45:28

• The Ten Commandments—Exodus 20:1-17

• The Lord is my shepherd—Psalm 23

• Christmas stories—Matthew 1–2; Luke 2:1-20

• The baptism of Jesus—Matthew 3:13-17; Mark 1:9-11; Luke 3:21-22; John 1:29-34

• The Easter Story—Matthew 26–28; Mark 14–16; Luke 22–24: John 13–21

• The Last Supper and Holy Communion—Matthew 26:17-30; Mark 14:22-26; Luke 22:7-20

• Jesus and the children—Matthew 19:13-15; Mark 10:13-16; Luke 18:15-17

• The Great Commandment—Matthew 22:34-40; Mark 12:28-31; Luke 10:25-28

• The Beatitudes—Matthew 5:1-12; Luke 6:20-23

• The Lord's Prayer—Matthew 6:9-13; Luke 11:2-4

- The Golden Rule—Matthew 7:12; Luke 6:31
- The Good Samaritan—Luke 10:25-37
- Love—1 Corinthians 13
- The Great Commission—Matthew 28:18-20

Is it important for children to memorize Scripture? Here are a few ideas to help you deal with this issue:

- Children will be more likely to want to learn Scripture if they see that it is something their parents know and love.
- Memorization of Scripture is most meaningful when it evolves as a natural process and can be related to a Bible story or life experience.
- Songs, sung over and over, are a fine avenue through which children can learn Scripture.
- Consistent exposure to the Bible is one of the best tools for memorization.
- "Knowing is more than memorizing. Being faithful is more than having the right words. Familiarity with faith language is important, but its contribution to growth in faith is one among many" (From *Helping Children Grow in Faith,* by Ruth McDowell and Crystal Zinkiewicz; copyright © 1990 Cokesbury; pamphlet).

WHEN QUESTIONS ARISE

As you strive to familiarize your children with the Bible, there will be many occasions when questions or concerns to which you have no answer arise. This has certainly been my experience! I have found that the best way to handle these situations is to

- admit that I do not know and suggest that we check with another source (a book, a pastor, and so forth);
- explain to my child that there are some things that only God knows and that we have to trust that God loves us and knows what is best for us.

The advice of Rabbi Marc Gellman and Monsignor Thomas Hartman in their book *Where Does God Live? Questions and Answers for Parents and Children* is also helpful. They say, "Don't be afraid to say 'I don't know' when talking to

> Songs, sung over and over, are a fine avenue through which children can learn Scripture.

your child about God. It is important for children to try to understand something that cannot be completely understood. God is real but complex. The message that not all reality is easy to understand is an important message. It will lead to curiosity and further reflection rather than to frustration and confusion. Try to follow any statements of what you don't *know* with statements of what you *believe*. The truth of the matter is that when a child asks you about God, he or she is asking not only about God but also about you" (Triumph/Liguori Publications, 1991; page 20).

LIVE THE BIBLE THROUGH YOUR EXAMPLE

Perhaps the most challenging and rewarding way to offer our children hands-on opportunities for experiencing the Bible is to live the Bible with our children. In other words, guide them to translate the words of the Bible into actions. Let us begin by looking at several key verses of Scripture to give us direction in how we might accomplish this.

In Matthew 22:37-38, Jesus instructs us with these words, " 'You shall love the Lord your God with all your heart, and with all your soul, and with all your mind.' This is the greatest and first commandment." We are given the Golden Rule in Matthew 7:12, "In everything do to others as you would have them do to you; for this is the law and the prophets." The Great Commission is found in Matthew 28:19-20, "Go therefore and make disciples of all nations, baptizing them in the name of the Father and of the Son and of the Holy Spirit, and teaching them to obey everything that I have commanded you. And remember, I am with you always, to the end of the age." Finally, reflect on 1 Corinthians 13:13, "And now faith, hope, and love abide, these three; and the greatest of these is love."

God is love, and love is at the heart of each of these verses. Living our lives in loving response to God's abundant and everlasting love for us is central to the teachings of the Bible. How, then, do we translate this message to our children? How do we help our children "live love"?

Let me suggest that children first need the inner assurance that they are loved. This becomes the basis for love of self, of others, and of God. Dwell on these thoughts to help your children sense that they are loved:

- The words children need to hear more than any other words are *You are loved; God loves you; I love you; Others love you.* Say these words any way you can and as often as you can. In the Downing family we have a unique way of saying "I love you." We squeeze each other's hand three times. It is something my husband told me about from his childhood, and something we as parents began doing with Julie when she was a young child.

- Make the loving decision to have your children baptized into the community of faith. This act results in their being surrounded by caring people who commit to love them and who give you support in affirming God's love for them.

- Repeatedly sing songs to and with your children. Such songs as "Jesus Loves Me," "Jesus Loves the Little Children," "He's Got the Whole World in His Hands," and countless others let children know they are loved.

- Read to your children and point out to them verses from the Bible and stories that give them the realization that God loves them. One of the most recognized of these verses is found in Matthew 19:14: "But Jesus said, 'Let the little children come to me, and do not stop them; for it is to such as these that the kingdom of heaven belongs.' " Read the book *The Runaway Bunny,* by Margaret Wise Brown, to your child; then talk with your child about how God's love for him or her is like the love of the mother bunny in the story, who is always there to love her child wherever he may be.

- Realize the lasting value of touch. Jesus did not keep the children at a distance. He drew them close to him. Rock and cradle your infant in your arms. Put your arm around a young child or hold the young child in your lap as you communicate with him or her. Be generous with hugs to children of any age.

- Reinforce the words of love you speak with loving actions. Give the gift of spending genuine time with your children. It will reveal more to them about how they are loved than any material thing ever could. It will also give your family precious memories of moments together that are irreplaceable!

The words children need to hear more than any other words are *You are loved; God loves you; I love you; Others love you.*

- Search out and emphasize the good in your children. Couple this with regular doses of praise and encouragement to let children know your love for them.

- Remember that we make children aware that they are loved through discipline. The Book of Proverbs tells us:

> Train children in the right way,
> and when old, they will not stray.
> (Proverbs 22:6)

Love is taking the time to give children guidelines and responsibilities. How can we expect our children to follow Jesus' example and the commandments God gives us, if they grow up with a lack of loving discipline at home?

- Pray that your children will feel God's love in their hearts and know that God loves them. Let your children hear you praying for them and thanking God for them.

- Join and become actively involved in a church of your choice. Through Sunday school, other programs, and the example of committed Christians, your children will be taught and made to feel secure in the knowledge of God's love for them.

- Write your child a letter at his or her birth and baptism, telling your child about these significant events. Describe feelings, who was present, and other meaningful thoughts and information, and perhaps include pictures. Let your child be aware of all the love generated during these special times. Save the letters to give to your child at a later stage of his or her life.

A second important premise for teaching our children to live love or live the words of the Bible is to set a loving example for them. Children are keen observers, especially of adults. Their actions frequently mimic those of their parents or other adults close to them. Be an example of love for your children by trying the following:

- Let your children see you reaching out in love to others as you carry food to a grieving family, visit a sick friend in the hospital, participate in Meals on Wheels or other programs that take food to people limited in their ability to leave their homes, greet a new neighbor, or respond to any of the numerous opportunities that come our way daily. Involve your children in these acts of love whenever you can.

- Allow your children to assist you in baking for someone, create their own get-well cards, accompany you on a visit, or pray with you for someone.

- When talking *about* or *to* someone else, speak loving words about these people for your children to hear. Jim's father tells this story about his own father, whom people called Uncle Mon. People would say of Uncle Mon, "You don't ever go into his home without leaving feeling good!" and "Uncle Mon never says a bad word about anyone." Unfortunately, I never met Jim's grandfather, but I believe those statements because they so accurately describe what Jim's dad was like. When we gossip, impose judgment on others, and say hurtful things, we teach our children to do the same.

- Teach your children the language of forgiveness by being forgiving yourself. Love and forgiveness are bound together. As parents, Jim and I have always tried to impress on Julie that while we might not like what she has done, we forgive her and will always love her. This underscores a valuable teaching from the Bible about God—that God's love is everlasting and that nothing can ever separate us from God's love.

- Live lives of acceptance. We believe that God accepts and cares for each person. Believing this, we strive for love and acceptance of others.

Prejudice, which is at the root of many of our world problems today, is a learned response. Children are not born with this quality. The Bible teaches that God's love is inclusive. We are all God's children. It is so important that we exemplify this attitude for our children through both our words and actions. Think what a different place this world would be if we all viewed one another as children of God. We can begin with ourselves!

In setting loving examples for our children, recognize that we often make the greatest impact through our daily, seemingly small acts of kindness as opposed to "scattered" major ones. Taking the time to help someone in need, sending a note, visiting a friend, listening to your child, or spending moments together as a family speaks clearly to our children about God's presence in our lives.

Let your children hear you praying for them and thanking God for them.

As we attempt to show our children how God wants them to live, let us remember to look to the biblical stories of Jesus and ask ourselves, "What would Jesus do?" and then to pray that we answer in such a way as to give our children glimpses of Jesus.

EXPERIENCE GOD'S WONDERFUL CREATION

Another important way that we live the Bible with our children is through caring for all of creation. Acknowledge and affirm that God is the Creator of humankind and of the world we live in. Celebrate together this glorious gift from God as you read the words from Genesis 1:1, "In the beginning when God created the heavens and the earth . . . "

Our family is blessed to have a cabin on Center Hill Lake, a beautiful retreat set within the hills of Tennessee. As a child, Jim went there with his family, and Jim and I have taken Julie there since she was an infant. When we are there, God's presence is so evident in all of nature that one feels that one could reach out and touch God. Nature and all of God's creation beckon us to realize the wonder of God.

There are endless opportunities for parents to foster an awareness and love of God's world with their children. Unlike the material possessions that we have to go out and purchase, and that eventually lose their appeal for our children, nature is ever present, always changing, forever there waiting to be discovered.

When our daughter was very young, she would stand at our back door and say, "Outside! Outside!" Think of nature as God's way of "knocking on our doors" to say, "Come be with me. Come know me." What are some ways we can help our children experience the outdoors and, in so doing, help them experience God?

When your children are young, begin to explore the wonders of God's world with them. Young children, especially, are drawn to the outdoors and fascinated with living things. They are full of questions and eager to observe and learn. If we reinforce and build on this interest, we will help them grow in their love of God and their caring for all of creation.

There are many wonderful children's books centered around nature. Take your child to a nearby park, spread a blanket and sit under a big tree in your yard, or find some other inspirational outdoors place to read a story with your child.

In her book *God Must Like to Laugh,* Helen Caswell says,

> God made the world—the heavens, too—
> And night and day, and me and you.
> But along with big things like the sun,
> God must have had a lot of fun
> Attending to each small detail:
> The fragile shell upon the snail,
> The flowers fitted to the bee,
> And little bugs too small to see.

> (Copyright © 1987 by Abingdon Press. Used by permission.)

Another book with a beautiful message is *God's Quiet Things,* by Nancy Sweetland. When you finish reading this story together, take the time to invite your child to be still, listen, and identify the sounds of God's world!

Look with your children at some of the psalms that tell of God's marvelous works! Read Psalm 104:24:

> O LORD, how manifold are your works!
>   In wisdom you have made them all;
>   the earth is full of your creatures.

Then take a walk together outdoors to search for God's creatures.

Before putting your child to bed at night, take him or her to a spot to observe the moon and stars. Read Psalm 8:3-4 and 8:9 with your child:

> When I look at your heavens, the work of your fingers,
>   the moon and the stars that you have established;
> what are human beings that you are mindful of them,
>   mortals that you care for them?
> O LORD, our Sovereign,
>   how majestic is your name in all the earth!

Then pray a prayer of thanks for God's world.

Acknowledge and affirm that God is the Creator of humankind and of the world we live in.

Reading the Bible With Our Children

Celebrate the changing of the seasons with your children. Learn to appreciate these changes with all your senses. Delight in the signs of new life that burst forth in the spring. Look for buds on the trees, flowers in bloom, fuzzy caterpillars, and butterflies. Listen for birds singing and bees buzzing. Praise and thank God with the hymn "All Things Bright and Beautiful":

> All things bright and beautiful,
> all creatures great and small,
> all things wise and wonderful:
> the Lord God made them all.
> Each little flower that opens,
> each little bird that sings,
> God made their glowing colors,
> and made their tiny wings.

> (By Cecil Frances Alexander; reprinted from *The United Methodist Hymnal,* copyright © 1989 The United Methodist Publishing House; 147.)

Here are some more ideas for helping your children explore God's world and grow in their love of God and creation:

• Plant a garden of flowers or vegetables with your children. Work with them and show them how to tend their garden, then together watch it grow!

• Fly a kite and talk with your child about how God is like the wind. We cannot see God, but we can feel God with us.

• Put on boots and rain gear and take a walk with your child in a spring rain. Play in the puddles. Be aware of how green and fresh everything looks. Always look for a rainbow after the rain!

• Enjoy a picnic and have some of your family devotionals outdoors during the summer. Thank God for the sunshine and the warmth it brings!

• Go barefoot with your children and feel God's world. Walk in the soft grass. If you live near the ocean or visit the beach, walk at the water's edge. Squish your toes in the sand. Recognize that these elements of nature are gifts from God!

• Go on a "treasure walk" with your child. Collect colored leaves, nuts, and other treasures that God uses to remind us that fall is here! Feel the air getting cooler! Notice the vibrant colors of God's world!

- If you live in an area where it snows, watch with your child for the first snowfall. Talk with your child about how God made each tiny snowflake different and special. Say: "God made you special too!" Go out and make footprints and angels in the snow.

- Creation is full of "surprises" just waiting to be found. Often the most treasured moments of worship we have with our children are the spontaneous ones. Ironically, it is frequently our children who alert us to these treasures. Look for a robin's egg, a ladybug, a bird's nest, a spider web, a squirrel carrying a nut, a rainbow, a star-filled sky, a snail's shell, spring's first crocus, and say thanks to God.

- Encourage your children to give creative expression to their feelings about God's world through artwork, poetry, a prayer, a song, or a story. Invite your children to show and tell about their creations as part of a family worship time. Children might also be willing to tell what they have done at Sunday school or with other church-related groups.

- When your family discovers a rainbow, read the story of Noah and the ark with your children. Talk about all of God's creatures who lived on the ark, how it rained and rained, and how God finally sent a dove with an olive branch as a sign to Noah that the rain would stop. Say: "When it stopped raining, God gave the world a rainbow as God's promise of love and hope forever!" Celebrate God's promise with a prayer of praise and thanksgiving.

- Pick a bouquet of wildflowers or flowers that you and your children have planted. Enjoy them yourselves, or give them to someone who is unable to get outside often, such as a nursing home resident, a hospitalized person, or people who are limited in their ability to leave their home.

- If you have a vegetable garden, invite your children to pick vegetables with you, help cook them, and then thank God for them when you have your blessing at mealtime.

- Set aside a place in your child's room or another place in your home to display outside treasures such as a bird's nest, pretty rocks, a robin's egg, a four-leaf clover, and other interesting finds!

- Consider allowing your child to have a fish aquarium or an indoor pet such as a hamster. Talk with your child about how these are God's creatures, too!

Often the most treasured moments of worship we have with our children are the spontaneous ones.

BE STEWARDS OF CREATION

When your children are young, begin helping them understand how all of creation is a gift from God, and that it is up to each one of us to take care of what God has so lovingly given to us. Say: "In caring for God's world, we are showing our love and appreciation to God." Speak these words often as your children grow. More importantly, though, reinforce your words with actions so that caring for God's world becomes a natural part of your family's life and not something done sporadically.

Pray together as a family and ask God to show you ways to be good stewards of our world, then decide on actions each family member—from youngest to oldest—can do to help. Recycling can involve the entire family. Taking time to pick up trash that is littering your neighborhood or another area in your community is a worthwhile family project.

Our church initiated a program whereby families could "adopt" a spot on the church grounds that needed beautification. Since its conception, flowers, potted gardens, and several trees have positively transformed many areas around our church. The families also commit to continually care for their adopted spots.

Teach your children to care for God's creatures by placing bird feeders in your yard. Give your children the responsibility for putting birdseed in the feeders. Watch the birds with your children and rejoice together over one of the miracles of God's creation. Julie loved to go with her grandfather to feed the ducks that lived in a pond in a nearby park! They would take a loaf of bread and spend a whole afternoon in an activity that delighted and entertained them both!

Use "earth friendly" products in your home whenever possible, and give your children the reason for their use. Say: "We help and love God by not wasting what we have been given!" Wherever your family is or wherever your family goes, do not be tempted to pollute God's world by throwing trash in a stream, along the road, or in any other inappropriate place. If you do it, your children will follow your lead.

WE ARE CREATED BY GOD

We cannot emphasize enough to our children that their lives are a gift from God, and that God created each one of them unique. Taking care of God's creation encompasses taking care of our bodies and minds, and this is an important means of showing our love for God. When we abuse ourselves, we are abusing God. We instill this belief in our children by exposing them to the church and the Bible, by lifting them up to God in prayer, and by setting a positive example in our homes. We instill this belief in our children by loving them and helping them feel good about themselves in every way we can! We cannot accomplish this task solely on our own, but the process must begin, and begin early, at home.

AWAKEN THE CHILD IN YOURSELF

Living the Bible with our children should result in

- giving children the inner assurance that they are loved;
- setting a loving example;
- acknowledging and affirming with them God's hand in all of creation.

Matthew 18:1-5 offers to us a fourth and wonderful way to live the Bible with our children. Listen to these words: "At that time the disciples came to Jesus and asked, 'Who is the greatest in the kingdom of heaven?' He called a child, whom he put among them, and said, 'Truly I tell you, unless you change and become like children, you will never enter the kingdom of heaven. Whoever becomes humble like this child is the greatest in the kingdom of heaven. Whoever welcomes one such child in my name welcomes me.' "

Jesus tells us that we must awaken the child in ourselves to truly live the Bible with our children. May the following prayer help you envision and renew the child in you.

We cannot emphasize enough to our children that their lives are a gift from God, and that God created each one of them unique.

AWAKEN THE CHILD WITHIN ME

Lord,
Awaken the child within me.
Let me look upon your world with a renewed sense of
awe and wonder.
Give me the eyes of a child so that I can experience the
miracles of creation as if for the first time.

Awaken the child within me.
Let me step out into your world and live my life with a
quiet trust in things unseen.
Grant me the feet of a child so that I can walk in faith with
the constant assurance that you are guiding me.

Awaken the child within me.
Let me reach out into your world and minister to each of
your children freely and unconditionally.
Bestow on me the arms of a child so that I can wrap them
around a troubled world and be a witness of your
everlasting love for us.

Awaken the child within me.
Let me gaze upon the face of baby Jesus, your Light to the
world.
Give me the heart of a child so that the promise of hope is
rekindled anew.

Awaken the child within me.
Let me recapture the true essence of wonder, faith, love,
and hope!
Let me discover and enter the kingdom of God.
Amen.

(From *Prayers for the Seasons of Life*, by Sue Downing,
copyright © 1997 by Sue Downing; published by
Providence House Publishers; pages 57 and 58.)

WHEN WE READ THE BIBLE WITH OUR CHILDREN,

- we recognize it as the Word of God and the story of God's love for us;
- we realize that not one of us ever ceases the need to grow in our understanding of the Bible, and that we are all forever learners;
- we see the importance of the Bible becoming a hands-on book within our families;
- we give our children Bibles, set loving examples for them, and attempt to live out the teaching of the Bible with them;
- we talk with our children about the Bible and why it is important to us;
- we help children understand how Bible teachings apply to today's situations;
- we listen with love to what our children have to say about the Bible.

ATTENDING CHURCH WITH OUR CHILDREN

Lord, we come before you in prayer for our children.

Help us to lovingly reach out, clasp their hands, and draw them ever nearer to you.

Awaken in us the need to become an active part of the community of faith.

One early spring afternoon at Brentwood Church Day School, I had taken my lively group of three- and four-year-olds out to our playground to release some energy. As I was pushing four-year-old Shannon on the swing, she suddenly turned her head, looked at me with a big smile, and said proudly, "Miss Sue, this is my church, and I share it with everybody!" While I listened to what Shannon was saying, several thoughts came to mind. I thought of Isaiah's words, "And a little child shall lead them" (Isaiah 11:6). How often we become the learners and our children the teachers. As Shannon's swing slowed to a halt, I gave her a big hug and said, "You are absolutely right!" Then I prayed a silent prayer of thanks to God for the church and for all the people who had touched my life and the lives of my family through the church.

As I told you previously, my husband, Jim, and I were fortunate to have parents who exposed us to the life of the church throughout our childhood. Through our experiences we learned the significance of making the church an integral part of one's family life. As we continue to grow and mature, we are made increasingly aware of the truly priceless gift we received. It is a gift that never stops giving and blessing our lives.

WHAT IS THE CHURCH?

Let us now examine more closely the importance of church. In a world where everything seems to be programmed for "fast forward and overdrive," why should families make the additional effort to belong to a church? What is it that sets church apart from all our other involvements?

The church is the Christian community of faith. It is a fellowship of believers who join together for the purpose of studying God's Word and helping one another grow in our faith. It is where we learn what it means to be children of God, and the tremendous privilege and responsibility that come with that "inheritance." The church is where we affirm through holy baptism that our children belong to God, and commit with the entire Christian community to help nurture them in the Christian faith. It is where we go to be fed spiritually.

We call the church the house of God. When we enter through its doors, we find a sanctuary where we can worship the one and only God, who created us and loves us more than we can ever imagine! We discover a place where we can search out God's will for our lives. We find a refuge where we can participate in the Lord's Supper through Communion and know that our sins are forgiven and that Jesus is always with us. Within the church walls, we can lay all we are, have been, and hope to be at God's altar. We can place our children in God's loving hands.

The church is you and me. God created each one of us as a unique person with significant gifts and talents. There is so much work to be done through the church, and God needs what we have to offer. Paul compared the church to a body, where each part is dependent on the other and every part makes a significant contribution to the working of the whole body. We give of ourselves not because it is "the thing to do," because we feel we have to, or because we are trying to earn credits toward our salvation. We do what we do to honor God and further God's kingdom here on earth. When we serve God through the church, we are blessed abundantly in ways we could never have imagined. When we are active participants in the life of the church, we are setting an example for our children. We are teaching them that the church needs each one of them, also.

The church is reaching out in love to others. A well-known children's fingerplay goes something like this:

This is the church.
This is the steeple.
Open the doors.
Out come all the people!

We come to church so that we can go out into the world for God. The church equips and sensitizes us to the countless ways we can accomplish this. The Christian church is not meant to be an exclusive club that is totally wrapped up in itself. The church knows no boundaries when reaching out in love to others. God is love, and God commands us to "love one another" (John 13:34). What better way to teach our children about God's love!

The church calls us to commitment. We choose to commit ourselves to God. God does not force us. Our commitment includes being faithful to God's church and the furthering of God's kingdom. We commit to nurture our children in the Christian faith through holy baptism.

The church is a place of hope. "God so loved the world that he gave his only Son, so that everyone who believes in him may not perish but may have eternal life" (John 3:16). The church is where we learn of hope for a troubled world. The church offers hope through God's love for each one of us. The church is a sanctuary of hope for the children. Without hope, there is not life.

FINDING A CHURCH HOME

We have looked at the importance of church and making it a part of our lives. Let us now examine the selection process for a church. How do we know if a church is "right" for our family? What are some helpful guidelines? First, it is good to note that there is great comfort in the realization that the church has no membership limits or time deadlines for join-ing. It is never too late for a family to become members of a church. Doing so is the most loving, positive decision you will make for the spiritual well-being of your family.

If your family is searching for a church as the result of a move or other such experience, or if your family is seeking

The Christian church is not meant to be an exclusive club that is totally wrapped up in itself. The church knows no boundaries when reaching out in love to others.

out a church for the first time, let your decision be guided by the following actions and criteria.

Make selecting a church a family decision

Where a family chooses to attend church will affect family members from infant to adult. Be intentional about involving your children in the decision-making process. Little ones as young as two to three years old can be included in times of family prayer, when you ask God's guidance in locating the right church for your family. They are also able to under-stand the concept that it is important to belong to a church because church is a special place where we go to learn about and worship a God who loves us tremendously! Older children can be invited to describe their impressions of a church. How did they feel about their Sunday school experi-ence and other programs such as choir, a children's mission club, vacation Bible school, or other opportunities you encouraged them to participate in. Assure your children that their feelings are an important part of the decision-making process, then truly listen and consider what they have to say. This not only results in a much smoother transition into a new church but also helps the children feel a real part of the church that your family will eventually join.

Pray for God's direction

Trust God to place your family where you need to be. As a young couple with a recently purchased first home, my hus-band and I were seeking a church home close to the Concord area of Knoxville, Tennessee, where we had just moved. Our daughter was one year old at the time. Over a period of about four months, we visited various churches, always ask-ing God to lead us to "our church." We joined Cokesbury United Methodist, where we became actively involved in its ministry. The impact on our lives and the life of that church was not fully realized until several years later when we expe-rienced the tragic death of our infant son, Scottie. The out-pouring of love from Cokesbury Church is difficult to describe. It transformed all our lives from then on. At the time, the church had been experiencing some of the growing pains that no church manages to escape. Scottie's death seemed to draw people's attention away from these problems and unite them in the common purpose of responding in love to a hurting family. At Scottie's memorial service, Jerry Anderson, our pastor at that time, said in his message: "In the few short weeks of Scottie's life, he has opened doors to an outpouring of love in our church and community. A little child has led us into new dimensions of loving and caring, and because of that we will never be the same." I tell you this story because I am convinced that God led us to Cokesbury Church at that particular time in our lives. God, in God's infinite wisdom, knew we needed Cokesbury Church and Cokesbury Church needed our family. When we choose to allow God to lead us, we will know in our hearts what is right to do and will be greatly blessed in our decision.

Locate area churches that your family could visit

Gather information on worship, Sunday school times, and other programs that your family might want to attend throughout the week. Once you begin visiting, it is a good idea to designate a place at your home to keep worship bulletins, program information, church newsletters, written reaction, and other pertinent information collected or sent to you by the churches. Plan to make at least several visits to all these churches. Many churches will make follow-up visits to your home. This is an excellent opportunity for your family to ask any questions you might have.

Determine the accessibility of a church. If one's church is located too far from one's home, it often becomes a chore to get a family there for Sunday morning worship, much less for other offerings throughout the week. It opens the possibility that children will not be attending church with children who go to their school. This in no way implies that it is never desirable to join a church at a distance from you, but it is a caution to give during this serious consideration.

Look for a church that you feel will meet the needs of your family. But equally important, look for a church where you feel that your family can make a real contribution. As I will discuss in more detail later in this chapter, church membership lacks all meaning if we view it only with the attitude, What can the church give or do for me?

> Look for a church that you feel will meet the needs of your family. But equally important, look for a church where you feel that your family can make a real contribution.

Be mindful that a "healthy" church will have a strong emphasis on outreach. This encompasses not only reaching out in love and support to the immediate membership but also extending that ministry to others out in the community and world at all age levels. Loving God and loving one another as God loves us should be the central focus of any church regardless of size, location, or budget.

Make a decision

Do not make a hasty decision, but make a decision. It can become a comfortable habit to continue attending numerous churches or "visiting" one church without ever taking the final step to actually join. When we fail to make a full commitment, we are cheating ourselves, our children, the church, and God. In a time of escalating mobility, a church home can give families, and especially our children, a sense of roots and a source of support and stability unlike any other institution.

BECOMING A PART OF THE CHURCH FAMILY

Once the step is made to join a church, it then becomes our responsibility to make the transition from joining to actually belonging, in every sense of the word. Many families join and attend the worship services but never really "belong" because of their lack of involvement. This reduces church membership to something that never reaches beyond the surface level. As I stated earlier, even before we join a church we should be asking ourselves, "What particular needs can we meet in this church? Where does each person in my family fit in?" It is only when we approach church membership with this kind of attitude that we honestly will experience the joy and fulfillment of belonging to a church.

We can help our children become a real part of church life by involving them in Sunday school, worship, vacation Bible school, children's choir, and numerous other programs that a church might offer throughout the week. This teaches them the importance of being active in church and the idea that church is not something we "do" only on Sundays. It gives our children the precious opportunity to learn about God and God's everlasting, abundant love for them.

As your children become older, you can encourage them to help in the church nursery, make posters for the church, be involved in an acolyte program, or minister in other ways. All these activities reinforce the idea that this is truly their church, too, and that they can make a worthwhile contribution to it.

As parents this effort is significantly "watered down" if we involve our children but do not involve ourselves. When we do not involve ourselves, we are saying, "These things are fine to do as children but are not that meaningful for adults." We teach our children best by our actions. I am blessed to have a wonderful mother who set a fine example for my brother and me in many areas, including church involvement. As far back as I can remember, I can picture my mother teaching Sunday school, creating posters and bulletin boards for the church, heading the Christian education commission, and doing countless other activities. In her later years she is still serving God through the church. I clearly recall thinking as a child, "I want to minister for the church in the same manner as my mother does." I can also picture how much it meant to me and how proud I was when my mom taught *my* Sunday school class or *my* vacation Bible school class.

My husband, Jim, remembers his father's deep commitment to the church. Jim's mother tells the story of how Jim, as an eight-year-old, witnessed his dad going to church so much that he asked her, "Mommy, is Daddy a minister?"

While I have chosen these specific examples to tell you, please understand, as I said earlier, that both our mothers and our fathers exemplified the importance of church involvement for us, and ideally this is how it should be. Children need to see active church participation from parents and other significant adults in their families, both male and female. One excellent way to provide a good example to your child is to teach your child's Sunday school class. In two-parent households, this provides a wonderful opportunity for mothers and fathers to do something together in a time when they are frequently heading in different directions.

There is a couple who is deaf in our church. They have two children whose hearing is normal. These parents are intensely

> Loving God and loving one another as God loves us should be the central focus of any church regardless of size, location, or budget.

committed to the church. Recently they offered to teach a sign language class to all who were interested. What a beautiful witness to their children of the power of God's love at work in their lives.

In any church a wide range of needs will surface, and you can choose to respond or not to respond to those needs. Often God's call invites us to minister in areas with which we are unfamiliar or have had little experience, such as teaching a children's Sunday school class. I offer this prayer to guide you as you consider your decision.

HERE I AM—I WILL TRY

Lord, You have called me to minister in a way I never
    have before.
I feel so inadequate for this task.
My qualifications are few, and my reasons to say no are
    many.
Are You sure You have connected with the right
    person?
Maybe You need to talk with a more likely candidate.

Lord, You have called me to minister in a way I never
    have before.
I feel afraid and unsure of what to expect and of what I'm
    to do.
What if I don't like the job I'm involved with? What if I'm
    a failure?
What if? What if?
Lord, it's not too late to say no, is it?

Lord, You have called me to minister in a way I never
    have before.
I am overwhelmed by the mere thought of what you have
    asked me to do.
It requires considerable time and effort to walk on unfa-
    miliar ground.
How about letting me choose something else to help you
    with that feels more comfortable?

Lord, You have called me to minister in a way I never
    have before.
You say that You will be with me each step of the way.
You ask me to remember Moses and countless others who
    thought that they were the wrong persons to serve.
You remind me that I'm the one you want, in spite of all
    my excuses.

Lord, You have called me to minister in a way I never
   have before.
Hesitantly, I take that first step of faith.
Here I am, Lord. I will try.
Amen.

When we trust God's guidance as we venture into new territory, we not only grow in our own faith but also set a wonderful faith example for our children!

The importance of giving

Good church stewardship encompasses not only the giving
of our time and talent but also the offering of our monetary
support. The pattern of giving that parents establish and set
as an example will touch their children's lives significantly
and will often determine how faithful children grow to be in
their giving. Many churches provide offering envelopes for
children to make a weekly contribution to the church. Older
children and youth are sometimes given the opportunity to
pledge an amount of money to the church each year like the
adults do. Whatever the situation, parents need to teach their
children the importance of consistent giving throughout the
year. Children should be allowed opportunities to give.
Young children can readily understand that we give to show
our love for God and God's church and to help others.
Older children can begin to comprehend that giving is an
act God calls us to do, and that the Bible further teaches us
that we should tithe, or contribute one-tenth of what we earn
or have for God's work in the world.

I will never forget sitting alone as a young child of five at the
end of a pew during worship. I did this only while my father
participated as an usher to help collect the offering. Sitting
there, I was so proud to have my nickel all ready to place in
the offering plate just at the proper time. How hurt I was
when one of the ushers—not my father—came to my pew
and passed me by, probably thinking I had nothing to offer.
What a disservice we do to our children when we deny
them the gift of giving.

When we trust God's guidance as we venture into new territory, we not only grow in our own faith but also set a wonderful faith example for our children!

As a final thought, try to give your children specific tasks to perform to earn their own offering if they do not receive an allowance. This will enhance the meaning of their giving.

Worshiping together

A significant part of embracing the church is a commitment to consistent Sunday morning worship attendance and regular participation in a Sunday school class. Especially in this day and time, living up to this commitment has become increasingly difficult, primarily for several reasons. First, the secular world has increasingly infringed on "church time." A lot of businesses remain open on Sunday. Children's and adults' sports and other events are often scheduled throughout the day. Sunday is no longer viewed as sacred by many. Second, a majority of families are overscheduled, overcommitted, and overworked. Unfortunately, Sunday usually gets the overflow! Instead of attending worship, families choose to sleep in, catch up on chores, exercise a favorite hobby, or indulge in some other tempting diversion. The suggestion here is not that under no circumstances should a family miss church on Sunday. This is unrealistic. The suggestion is that families make attending worship a priority. No matter how much busyness fills our lives, we always manage somehow to do the things we really want to do. Regular church attendance is something families need to work at continuously. It is a discipline. Our family's experience has been that when we make the extra effort to go to church, even when we do not "feel" like it, we are always glad we did and always blessed.

When your family is vacationing or away from home for other reasons, consider worshiping in another church or planning a family devotional. These alternatives can draw your family close to God no matter where you are!

What if one parent chooses not to attend church at all? Jerry, the pastor of a church we formerly attended, relates this story. As a young married man, Jerry refused to go to church, but his wife faithfully went and took their young son with her. Sunday after Sunday this scenario repeated itself. Jerry's wife, Martha, never tried to force him. She simply set an example and prayed. Jerry eventually chose to attend church with his family, and he went on to answer God's call into the ordained ministry. This story teaches us to be determined in our church attendance, even if a spouse is not. It helps us see the value of patience, understanding, and faith in situations such as this. It also gives us a sense of hope and again shows what a remarkable teacher example is.

Besides bringing our children to Sunday morning worship, parents and other adults need to be supportive of and sensitive to the varied ways children can contribute to the worship experience. In other words, how can our worship services be more "child friendly"? Children can serve as acolytes, lighting the candles or assisting at offering time. Children can have the responsibility for collecting a special offering for missions. Children could sing at designated services. In our church an eleven-year-old boy has been invited several times to use his gift of music to play the postlude on our organ for the closing of the worship service. Children's Day is celebrated in many churches. This is a day on which the children are recognized and are given responsibility for the various parts of the worship service.

A growing number of churches devote a portion of their service to a children's message or a time when the children gather to hear a story and pray. Sometimes banners that children's classes have created are displayed in the narthex or sanctuary.

Through the sacrament of baptism we become members of the household of faith. Just as we welcome all family members at a family dinner, The United Methodist Church welcomes all members of Christ's family, regardless of their age, at the Communion Table.

All these things say to our children, "We love you. God loves you. You are welcome here!" This inclusiveness does not just happen. Again, we need to support and continually look for ways our children's presence can be reflected in the worship time. We must be advocates for our children.

Recognize too that the mere act of sitting together as a family in church not only enriches our faith but gives our children the opportunity to learn and grow in their faith. Church

> Besides bringing our children to Sunday morning worship, parents and other adults need to be supportive of and sensitive to the varied ways children can contribute to the worship experience.

attendance is not an option; it is a must for people seeking a Christ-filled, God-centered life for themselves and their children. To forfeit this privilege and responsibility is to spiritually starve our families. Jim's father was truly a man of God. The message he left on the answering machine in his family's home concluded with, "We hope you attend church Sunday." Let this message be a reminder and hope for each one of us!

Celebrating the church year

A meaningful part of belonging to the church is the celebration of special times throughout the church year. Family participation within the church and home during these times can give our children lasting memories and wonderful traditions to pass on to their children. How families celebrate these times and the emphasis we place on them can impact how our children view their faith. The seasons of the church year provide wonderful opportunities for remembering and celebrating God's love.

ADVENT

The word *Advent* comes from a Latin word that means "coming." The season of Advent is a time of waiting and preparation. It begins the fourth Sunday before Christmas Day and continues until Christmas Eve. It is a time to get ready for and anticipate the coming of God's son, Jesus. Advent leads us to a manger in Bethlehem. Unfortunately for many families, Advent has evolved into a hectic, stressful, overcommitted period of time that leaves them breathless by Christmas Day! It is in this kind of environment that the real meaning of Advent and Christmas is lost. Let us examine some ways to remove our families from "fast forward" and slow down to truly experience Advent with our children as we should and want to do.

Take time to pray

Pray individually. Pray as a family. Set aside moments for prayer when you ask God to guide you and help you in making the Advent season a holy time for your family. Prayer connects us with God, calms us, and causes us to be still.

Take time to decide

Before Advent is upon you, decide as a family what season-related activities you want to participate in. Be selective; do not try to do it all! The offerings at church that you do not choose to do this year will be a possibility for next year.

Take time to worship

Observe Advent together by lighting Advent candles at your home on the four Sundays before Christmas. Light the fifth candle on Christmas Day. Purchase or create your own family Advent wreath. Traditionally, the four Advent candles are purple, and the Christ candle is white and is placed in the center of the wreath. Family devotionals focused on the lighting of the candles can reflect the significance of the Advent wreath. Churches often have available suggestions for family home worship. Devotions can also be found in your child's Sunday school curriculum. Better yet, create your own!

Actively involve each family member in some way during this special time, such as in holding the Bible, helping to light a candle, or telling a blessing! Impart to your children that we also worship God by our loving actions. During a family Advent devotional, decide on some specific act of giving for your family to do for another family or individual, for example preparing a meal for them, inviting them to a special church service, or offering to run errands for them. Then lift this activity up in prayer as a gift to God!

Take time to give

Central to this season should be thoughts of giving and doing for others. One of the most rewarding experiences our family has had is delivering food baskets and packages to families in need. I also recall another experience in which our family had the privilege of taking money collected by our Sunday school class to a church family in which the father had been without work for some time. I do not think any of us will ever forget the feel of their hugs or the look of gratitude on the faces of that mother and father. There are endless opportunities to show love during the Advent season. Children delight in giving and watching others receive. I will always

The seasons of the church year provide wonderful opportunities for remembering and celebrating God's love.

remember the uncontained excitement in our daughter's eyes as she watched her daddy open the gift of a picture she had painted just for him.

Take time to make memories

Set up a Nativity scene in a prominent place in your home. If the Nativity scene is "untouchable," set up another one for your children to move the figures about and tell the Christmas story in their own words. Place the Nativity scene close to your Advent wreath to create an Advent worship center for your family.

Bake together. Let your children help make and decorate cookies to give to family, friends, or others. Help your children make homemade Christmas cards or gifts to give. These are the best gifts and do not have to be elaborate to be cherished!

Read with your children. Read or tell the Christmas story together over and over again. Many wonderful books also touch on the meaning of Christmas. Stories such as *Why Christmas Trees Aren't Perfect* help us and our children dwell on what Christmas is all about! Each Christmas I have given our daughter a new children's book that touches on the message of love that the season brings. I also include a note inside the book for her. She turned twenty-two this year and still receives this gift. Eventually she can share the books with her children or other children she comes to know.

Create or secure an Advent calendar to help your family count the days until Christmas. Making one can be as simple as cutting out star shapes or purchasing large star stickers and placing them on the day squares of a ready-made calendar.

Sing songs. Go caroling together. Sing Christmas hymns as part of your Advent devotionals or at a family gathering. Record these times on audiocassette or videocassette for cherished memories. We would not take anything for the family Christmas tape of Julie introducing "Jesus Loves Me" as her favorite Christmas carol!

Set aside a date to decorate the tree as a family. Rediscover beloved ornaments and the meaning they have. Play Christmas carols as you do this. When the tree is complete, turn out all the lights except those on the tree. Say a prayer of thanks to God for Jesus, the light of the world!

Attend church and allow your family to experience the church celebrations connected with Advent. Visit the sanctuary with your children when no one else is present. Look at the decorations. Gaze at the Chrismon tree. Obtain a description of the meanings of the Chrismon ornaments from your church or another source and explore the meanings with your children. Sense the wonder of the season. Kneel at the altar and pray a prayer of thanks to God.

Establish new traditions and practice old family ones. It would not seem like Advent and Christmas in our home if there were no German *stollen* to eat or if we did not attend the Christmas Eve candlelight service. Traditions bring families closer, provide precious memories for our children, and serve as gentle reminders of cherished times. Frequently traditions just happen and are not planned. This is what makes them special!

CHRISTMAS

Advent prepares us for the season of Christmas. The Christmas season begins on Christmas Eve or Day and lasts for twelve days. There are many ways to make this a celebration of the birth of our Savior rather than a secular holiday that focuses on getting presents. Amidst all the glitz and materialism that calls for our attention during this season, take time to keep your family's hearts fixed on a manger in Bethlehem where a tiny baby who was God's message of everlasting love to the world was born long ago. Remember that we always tend to take time for the things that we really want to do and that are important to us.

Make room in your "inn." Invite someone who will be without family during the holidays to spend Christmas Eve or Christmas Day with your family.

Each year, give your children a new ornament—such as a star, an angel, or a candle—that serves as a reminder of the Christmas story. Let them put these meaningful ornaments on

> Traditions bring families closer, provide precious memories for our children, and serve as gentle reminders of cherished times.

the family tree or a small tree of their own. Simple gestures such as these help a family remain focused on Jesus' birth.

Give your children the opportunity to place a poinsettia or other flower in the sanctuary in honor or memory of someone. Honor your children with a poinsettia as a gift of love. Help your children carry the message of love and joy that Christmas brings throughout the year. Christmas is a beginning, not an ending. Continue to exemplify and find with them ways to spread God's love!

SEASON AFTER THE EPIPHANY

The Epiphany is celebrated on the twelfth day after Christmas Day, January 6; and the season after the Epiphany continues until Lent begins. It is a time when we hear the story of how wise men came from the East and followed a star to bring gifts to the baby Jesus. The word *epiphany* means show forth. The visit of the wise men symbolizes God showing himself to all the world in the Christ child.

The Epiphany calls us as families to carry the message of love and joy that Christmas brings out into the world. It offers a wonderful opportunity to focus on the importance of the belief that we are all missionaries and that each of us has unique gifts to offer Jesus.

The Epiphany is a day when families can reflect on and give thanks for the many and varied gifts they have received. Let us now look together at some ways families can celebrate the day of the Epiphany.

• Read the story of the wise men as a family from Matthew's Gospel (2:1-12). Consider withholding the wise men figures from your Nativity scene until this time, then adding them as you read the story. Talk about the gifts that the wise men brought, which were fit for a king. Explore together what gifts of love each family member can offer for Jesus. Center on acts of kindness. Also think about gifts of love you could offer as a family.

• Gather your family outside to behold a star-filled sky. Search for one of the brightest stars you can see. Invite your children to tell the story of the wise men. Lift up a prayer of thanks to God for Jesus.

- Make star-shaped cookies with your children to celebrate the Epiphany. As you work together, talk about how the star reminds us of the wise men and how Jesus is the light of the world. Give the cookies to someone as a gift, or invite friends over to eat them with you.

- Read *The Christmas Star*, by Marcus Pfister, with your children. Then help them create shining stars to display in your home. Add glitter to cut-paper stars, or cover cardboard star shapes with bright foil paper.

- Sing or listen to carols in remembrance of the Epiphany. "We Three Kings" tells about this season in a beautiful way. Other appropriate hymns are "There's a Song in the Air," "We Would See Jesus," and "The First Noel." All of these are found in *The United Methodist Hymnal*. Also be aware of the hymns sung during church worship during this time.

- Take time to look again at cards and pictures your family has received. Pray a prayer of thanksgiving for each family represented. Ask that God's loving presence be with these families throughout the coming year.

- Encourage your children to express their thanks to individuals for the gifts they have been given. Young children can dictate words of thanks for you to write and send, or they can create a picture of thanks. Older children can write their own notes. Remember too that parents who show thanks impress on their children the importance of giving thanks.

- Invite each family member to set aside a toy, book, or something else they own to give to a charitable organization in thanks for all they have received. Bring these gifts and place them near your family's Nativity scene. As you do, thank God for the gift of God's son, Jesus.

The season after the Epiphany emphasizes to us that Christmas is a beginning, not an ending. During these days we can help our children find ways to share the joyous news of Jesus' birth by spreading God's love. Here are a few suggestions:

- Give the gift of light. Collect a family offering or let your children earn money to give toward payment of the electric bill for a family in need.

- Let your children assist you in gathering winter clothes items—socks, mittens, caps, jackets, sweatshirts—that your

Christmas is a beginning, not an ending. Continue to exemplify and find with your family ways to spread God's love!

family no longer uses and donate them to the Salvation Army or other such organizations.

- Invite a new family in the neighborhood to attend church with you. Then have a meal together afterward.

- Discuss and commit to one new way each family member can minister to others through the church. Ask God to guide each family member in his or her decision.

- Allow your children to help prepare and package a meal for a family in need. Then deliver the food together. Talk with your children about the feelings they have when your family does this.

- Bring joy to one or more people who are confined indoors—such as someone who is hospitalized, a resident in a nursing home, or a neighbor who is unable to get out—by visiting them. Often the gift of our presence has more meaning than any other!

- Remember and give thanks for the birds during this time by feeding them. Let your children help you use a heart-shaped cookie cutter to cut shapes from day-old bread. Spread a thin layer of peanut butter on the bread and sprinkle bird seed on it. Use a toothpick to poke a hole through the top of the heart shapes. String a piece of yarn through the hole and tie it to create a loop. Then help your child hang the feeders on a tree or shrub for the birds to eat during winter months.

Through the celebration of the Advent and Christmas seasons, our families prepare for and rejoice over the birth of a baby in a lowly manger in Bethlehem. The season after the Epiphany focuses us on Jesus' life and ministry.

LENT

The Lenten season brings to mind a different kind of picture: that of Jesus on the cross. The word *Lent* originally meant spring. For the Christian church, Lent, which begins with Ash Wednesday, is the period of forty days before Easter, not counting Sundays. Lent is a special time to celebrate God's great love for us! Families can choose to worship God during Lent through sharing, giving, and caring. Parents can help their children know that loving others is one of the greatest gifts we can give to God. Parents can also use this season to teach their children that the small acts of kindness we perform day by day are sometimes the best.

Decide with your child on an act of kindness he or she can do for God during each of the forty days of Lent. You could write the ideas ahead of time or keep a record of them as they are done so that you and your child can reflect upon them. It is easy for parents to participate in this activity. Here are a few suggestions for you to build on. Adapt ideas to the age of your child.

- Pray for those who are sick and hungry. If possible, visit someone who is sick, and give food to someone who is hungry.
- Call or visit a family member or friend to say "I love you."
- Invite someone to go to church with you.
- Take a spring walk with someone.
- Have a family Lenten devotional each day. Tell your joys, what you are thankful for, and ways you showed God's love to others. Many churches offer daily Scripture to be read.
- Make an effort to look at your child's Sunday school leaflets or other seasonal materials brought home from church. These will be of great help as you attempt to impress on your child the significance of Lent.
- Make pretzels. The pretzel shape represents arms crossed in prayer. Traditionally many people gave up milk, eggs, and other fats during Lent. Since pretzels contain only flour, water, and salt, they provided a bread substitute during Lent.

Holy Week

As your children become older, they will gradually be able to better comprehend the sadness associated with the Lenten season. But they will also grow to understand how God took the sadness of Good Friday and transformed it into the joy and hope that Easter morning brings! Here are a few suggestions for things you can do to make Holy Week—the final week of Lent that leads to Easter Sunday—meaningful for the entire family:

- Many churches include a procession of children waving palm branches as a part of the worship service on Palm Sunday. Read the Palm Sunday story from the Bible with your children. Say how happy the people were to see and

> Decide with your child on an act of kindness he or she can do for God during each of the forty days of Lent.

welcome Jesus. Talk with your children about how we can welcome Jesus into our hearts today by loving others as Jesus did. Encourage your children to save their palm branches, if possible, as a reminder of this day.

• Bake or purchase hot cross buns for your family to eat together on Good Friday. Show your children the mark of the cross on this pastry. Say a prayer of thanksgiving for Jesus.

• Visit the sanctuary by yourselves, or attend the Good Friday service with your child. Experience the darkness and "emptiness" of the church. Then, three days later on Easter morning your child will see the church filled with joy, alleluias, and Easter lilies seeming to "trumpet" the good news: Christ is risen!

• Again look to nature with your children. Rejoice with them about how things that seemed barren and dead in the winter took on new life in the spring. Tell your children how God gives everything new life. Read with them the story *The Fall of Freddie the Leaf*, by Leo Buscaglia, which illustrates this in a beautiful way!

EASTER

Easter Sunday is the beginning of the Easter season, which lasts for fifty days. It is the most celebratory season of the church year. The Easter story, with Jesus' crucifixion, is a difficult story for children to understand. It is a story that we as parents tend to gloss over with our children. However, the Easter story is one of joy and hope! It carries with it the central message of the Christian faith. The good news is that Christ is risen, and through his resurrection our sins are forgiven and we have everlasting life! Establish family traditions that help emphasize the meaning of the Easter season. Here are a few suggestions:

• Choose to honor or remember another person with an Easter lily for your church. Let your child honor his or her Sunday school teacher, a family member, or a close friend with a lily; or honor your child with an Easter lily as a gift of love!

• Attend a sunrise Easter service.

• Make a family occasion of dying eggs. Talk with your children about how eggs are a visible sign of new life.

- Place in your child's Easter basket a gift that is a reflection of the Christian church—a new Bible or Bible storybook, a bookmark with a biblical message, a cross necklace or lapel pin.

- Help your children create their own Easter cards to send.

- Bake butterfly-shaped cookies to enjoy and to give away.

- Consider other ways for your family to observe this season of new life. Go for a spring walk or have a picnic outdoors together. Look for signs of new life—budding flowers and trees, green grass, butterflies, a robin's egg. Lift up a prayer of thanks and praise to God for these things!

- Read with your child *Tale of Three Trees*, a beautiful folk-tale for Christmas or Easter about the special wishes of three trees. The message is wonderful for readers of all ages. Read classic books—such as *The Golden Egg Book*, by Margaret Wise Brown, or *The Very Hungry Caterpillar*, by Eric Carle—that teach of new life. Then talk with your child about how the gift of new life comes from God.

Easter is an opportune time to help your older children begin to get a grasp for the meaning of two key Scriptures, Romans 8:28 and Romans 8:37-39. Their messages are that all things work together for good for those who trust in God, and that nothing can separate us from God's love. I cannot tell you the number of times I have looked to these Scriptures myself and have shared them with our daughter. What a wonderful sign of hope for our children as they grow into adulthood in a world where so many bad things seem to be happening. To help our children believe that God's love is with them in all the circumstances of life and that God can bring good from bad just as God did for Jesus, is a precious gift to give them. At Christmas we help our children focus their hearts on a manger in Bethlehem, where love was born. At Easter we help our children's hearts to be filled with joy and thanksgiving for God's gift of everlasting life to us!

SEASON AFTER PENTECOST

Easter leads us into another important time in the church year: the celebration of Pentecost, or the birthday of the New Testament church. Pentecost is celebrated on the fiftieth day after Easter, and the season after Pentecost continues

To help our children believe that God's love is with them in all the circumstances of life and that God can bring good from bad just as God did for Jesus, is a precious gift to give them.

until Advent begins. The story of Pentecost is found in the Book of Acts. It tells of a new power given to the first Christians following Jesus' resurrection. This power from God is the Holy Spirit. It is a power that is alive within the fellowship of believers today. The Holy Spirit is God working in and through us.

Parents can help their children recognize the action of the Holy Spirit in their lives and the life of their church. Children can also grow in the realization that they can be God's witnesses and help God's church continue to grow wherever they are.

Young children can be led to the understanding that God is always with us. Spend time talking with them about how God never leaves us. Say: "God stays with us no matter how we are feeling or what we have done. God is the best friend we will ever have. God shows us how to be more loving to others." All of this tells our children that they are never alone. God does not live in a far away place; God is always with us.

When children become older, they can further see that through the work of the Holy Spirit, God is forever guiding, teaching, and showing them opportunities to minister in love to others. They can understand that the church grows through the giving of God's love, and that we are all God's disciples. It is also important to impress on our children that God is not a God of force. God does not make us love others. We choose to love out of our love for God and God's children.

As our children grow and mature in their faith, we can also help them become aware of the special gifts or fruits that the Holy Spirit brings to us. Galatians 5:22-23 lists these as love, joy, peace, patience, kindness, generosity, faithfulness, gentleness, and self-control. We can share with our children that God's Spirit and the gifts it brings empower us and give us the responsibility to live lives pleasing to God.

Again, the season after Pentecost brings with it the joyful message that God is very much at work in our lives and the life of the church. This is a message our children need to hear over and over again. It is a message our children can begin to comprehend. It is a message we must live with our children when they are young.

The following are some specific ways for you and your children to observe the season after Pentecost and the good news it brings:

- Attend church together on Pentecost Sunday. Take time beforehand to explain to your children the celebration that will be taking place. When you enter the church sanctuary with your children, look for Pentecost banners or other signs of Pentecost, such as the flame. Point these out to your children, then set aside time to talk about them. Also observe with your children any other ways Pentecost is celebrated during the worship service.

- Invite your children to help you create a birthday cake in honor of the church's birthday. As you work, talk about and decide on a gift of love your family could give to the church—an offering to an outreach ministry, the gift of a book to the church library, the gift of a pew hymnal or Bible, the donation of your time to a church mission project, and so forth.

- Sing with your children the wonderful hymn "We Are the Church" (*The United Methodist Hymnal,* 558). Discuss with your children how the church is a family of people who believe in and follow Jesus. Say: "We are a part of God's family." If your church has a pictorial directory, take a moment to look at it together and talk about how these friends are all part of your church family.

- Look at pictures of your children at various ages and share memories from their birthdays with them. Point out how they have grown. Say: "Each one of us can help God's church grow by telling others about Jesus and God's love for them. We can do this best through loving others."

- Spend time outside with your children. Blow bubbles with them. Say: "God's Spirit is like the wind. We cannot see it, but we can feel it. God's Spirit is always with us, helping us feel loved, and helping us, in turn, love others." If bubbles are not available, observe wind blowing through the trees or the effect a gentle breeze has on wind chimes.

- Read and talk about the story of Pentecost with your children. Their Sunday school materials are an excellent

> Discuss with your children how the church is a family of people who believe in and follow Jesus.

resource for this. Depending on your children's ages, read the Pentecost story from the Book of Acts from a children's version of the Bible or from your family Bible. Allow time to discuss the significance of the Pentecost story with your children. Tell them how, on that Pentecost Sunday long ago when the church began, the apostle Peter preached the very first sermon. Let them know that three thousand people came to believe in Jesus and were baptized. Go on to explain how, on that very day, God gave to all believers the gift of the Holy Spirit, which is a gift each one of us has today. Explain that the Holy Spirit is God with us.

- Familiarize your children with the early history of Pentecost. Older children can look this information up on their own in a Bible reference book. Help your children discover how Pentecost was one of the celebrations of the Jewish people, observed with the wheat harvest fifty days after Passover. Make them aware that the Pentecost we read about in Acts took place fifty days after Jesus' resurrection.

- When you become aware of a crisis in your church, such as the death of a loved one, illness, loss of a job, or other tragedy, decide as a family one or more ways to respond in love to the people involved. Impress on your children that this is one of the most important responsibilities we have as a church family. Acknowledge and give thanks to God when church members support your family in times of need.

As we think about this season, let me say that the greatest avenue we have to celebrate and teach our children the true meaning of Pentecost is to actively live the message it brings. We accomplish this through regular church attendance, being actively involved in the community of faith, studying God's Word, upholding one another in times of sorrow, celebrating together at times of joy, recognizing and using our God-given gifts for God's glory, and allowing the Holy Spirit to lead us in all we do.

At Christmas we help our children focus their hearts on a manger in Bethlehem. At Easter we help our children gaze beyond the cross to an empty tomb and Christ's victory over death. At Pentecost we help our children understand the birth of the church and the gift of the Holy Spirit.

As we celebrate special times in the life of the church with our children, let us forever remember and teach them that each moment, each hour, each day in the life of the church is special and gives us opportunity to openly express our love to God.

Experiencing the sacraments

A discussion of attending church with our children would be incomplete without focusing on the sacraments of baptism and Holy Communion. These are two especially significant acts of worship that people experience within the church. How we guide our children to perceive these sacraments will have a lasting impact on their lives and the way they view God and God's house, the church.

BAPTISM

Baptism is a sacrament of inclusiveness; assurance; and, above all, God's grace. It signifies that we belong to the family of God. Through baptism we are eternally linked to God with Christians everywhere and are given the blessed assurance that the gift of God's Holy Spirit is and always will be with us. The loving decision to present our children for baptism in God's church is one of the greatest gifts we can give to them.

The United Methodist understanding of infant baptism is described in this statement: "The church affirms that children being born into the brokenness of the world should receive the cleansing and renewing forgiveness of God no less than adults. . . . The baptism of an infant incorporates him or her into the community of faith and nurture . . . Understanding the practice as an authentic expression of how God works in our lives, The United Methodist Church strongly advocates the baptism of infants within the faith community: 'Because the redeeming love of God, revealed in Jesus Christ, extends to all persons and because Jesus explicitly included the children in his kingdom, the pastor of each charge shall earnestly exhort all Christian parents or guardians to present their children to the Lord in Baptism at an early age' (1992 *Book of Discipline*, ¶ 221). We affirm that while thanksgiving to God and dedication of parents to the task of Christian

> Baptism is a sacrament of inclusiveness; assurance; and, above all, God's grace.

child-raising are aspects of infant baptism, the sacrament is primarily a gift of divine grace. Neither parents nor infants are the chief actors; baptism is an act of God in and through the church. . . . Since baptism is primarily an act of God in the church, the sacrament is to be received by an individual only once" (From *The Book of Resolutions of The United Methodist Church—1996.* Copyright © 1996 The United Methodist Publishing House; Used by permission; pages 727–728).

Baptism, while first and foremost an act of God's grace, is a sacrament through which parents or guardians, along with the entire Christian community of faith, are called by God to play an active role in helping to nurture and shape the spiritual growth of a child. Parents hold the key responsibility of making the decision to bring their children before God for baptism. In many congregations the parents also select sponsors or godparents for their children. These specially chosen people commit to drawing a child closer to God throughout that child's life. Traditionally, godparents participate with the parents in a child's baptism. Jim and I are the godparents for our niece Amy, and it has been a joy to be part of and witness the evolvement of her continued spiritual growth.

The baptismal service is a churchwide celebration. It is not meant to be a private ceremony. When a child is baptized, the whole faith community pledges to embrace that child with God's love. Listen to the words of the congregation's vow in The Baptismal Covenant II, *The United Methodist Hymnal*:

> With God's help we will proclaim the good news
>   and live according to the example of Christ.
> We will surround *these persons*
>   with a community of love and forgiveness,
>   that *they* may grow in *their* service to others.
> We will pray for *them*,
>   that they may be true disciples
>   who walk in the way that leads to life.

> (From "Baptismal Covenant II," in *The United Methodist Hymnal.*
> Copyright © 1976, 1980, 1985, 1989 The United Methodist
> Publishing House; page 40. Used by permission.)

Infants and young children cannot know what is happening for them through baptism, but as a child matures, the significance of this sacred event can be gradually imparted to him or her. Parents need to purposely take the time to talk with their child about his or her baptism. I offer these suggestions:

- In many congregations a significant part of the baptismal service is the lighting of the baptismal candle from the large paschal (Easter) candle. This candle is given to parents as a symbol of their child's baptism. Each anniversary of your child's baptism, relight the candle as a family and remind your child about his or her baptism. Say: "Baptism means that you belong to God and God's family." Young children can understand that Jesus, too, was baptized. Later on, children can understand that water is a symbol for baptism because all life depends on water.

- Create a scrapbook centered around your child's baptism. Include pictures of those present, the certificate of baptism, the worship bulletin, and any other mementos from that day. Write down your thoughts and feelings. Invite your pastor to contribute a brief message to your child. As well as being a cherished keepsake, this book provides a wonderful stepping stone for discussion of baptism with your child.

- When there is a baptism at your church, talk with your child about it after the worship service. Say: "You have been baptized, too!"

- Act out baptism as a family, using a child's doll. Invite family members to pretend to be the pastor, godparent, parent, and a member of the congregation.

- Visit the church sanctuary during the week. Show your child the baptismal font and talk about what takes place there.

- Tell your child about your own baptism and what it has meant to you.

- Read together from the Bible the story of Jesus' baptism in the Jordan River by John. This story is found in Matthew 3:13-17, Mark 1:9-11, Luke 3:21-22, and John 1:29-34.

As we present our children for baptism, let us be forever mindful that the most crucial thing we can do is faithfully live the vows made to God and our children. In so doing we nurture their spiritual growth as well as our own and help to perpetuate the family of God.

> When a child is baptized, the whole faith community pledges to embrace that child with God's love.

HOLY COMMUNION

Holy Communion is the other sacrament of the church that represents a sign of God's love for us. Communion is a loving reminder that Jesus is with us always. As families, we can experience through the bread and cup an extraordinary shared meal with Jesus and can realize the forgiveness of God's love.

John Wesley, the founder of Methodism, believed that all children, including the young, should be invited to the Communion Table. While many denominations practice this, there are those that believe that children must be confirmed first. In conjunction with this, let me relate a story that Judy Norris, our church children's coordinator, frequently tells. She talks about worshiping in church one Communion Sunday and observing the people going toward the altar to partake of Communion. As a mother and her young son walked by, Judy heard the boy say, "Oh, look at the bread. I love to eat bread." In reply the mother said, "No, you cannot have any. That bread is not for you." Judy goes on to describe the look of hurt and rejection that appeared on the boy's face. This story carries with it several lessons for us. First, it shows that churches need to be sensitive to the fact that families come from varied religious backgrounds and traditions. But second and foremost, it should prompt us as parents to examine our feelings about children and Communion.

A primary argument against young children taking Communion is that they do not understand what is happening. I affirm the views of Hoyt L. Hickman on this issue. In his article "Children and Communion" he says, "It is true that there is much about Holy Communion that children do not understand. After more than fifty years of experiencing Holy Communion and studying its many levels of meaning, there is much about it that I do not understand.

"Think about what a child does know. A small child already knows the difference between being accepted and rejected at a meal table. The child already connects being fed with being loved. Such experiences can help children know the Christ who accepts and loves us.

"Does a child have faith? Faith goes beyond intellectual belief and is rooted in trust. How trusting children are!" (From *Children's Bible Studies: Elementary B Teacher, Spring 1987;* copyright © 1986 Graded Press; page 76.) As Jesus said, "Let the little children come to me; do not stop them; for it is to such as these that the kingdom of God belongs" (Mark 10:14).

In reflection, I can recall the countless times Jim, Julie, and I have gone as a family to receive Communion. The church, circumstances, and method have not always been the same. But what has remained constant is the feeling of God's forgiving love, the awareness of Jesus' presence with our family, and a real sense of spiritual closeness with one another. Many times Communion has also given us the opportunity to kneel at the altar, clasp hands, and pray together as a family in God's house.

In talking with pastors and other church staff, and in my ministry with children, I have discovered that when children are asked what their favorite or most meaningful part of the worship service is, they frequently respond, "Communion." This suggests that children have far more insight than we adults often give them credit for, and it also hints that children have some understanding of the specialness of this sacrament.

To reinforce your child's understanding of the sacrament, look for moments to talk with your child about Communion. Perhaps this could happen before or after a Communion service. Help your child feel comfortable in participating in this sacrament by describing the logistics of Communion services in your church. You may even want to visit the sanctuary before a service and practice walking to the front of the church, kneeling at the rail, or other procedures related to Holy Communion. Be aware of when your child will be learning about Communion and the Last Supper in Sunday school, and use that learning as the basis for conversations with him or her. Discuss these thoughts with your child:

• Communion plays an important part in the worship service.

• Through communion we can remember the special meal that Jesus shared with his disciples long ago.

A small child already knows the difference between being accepted and rejected at a meal table. The child already connects being fed with being loved.

- Communion helps us feel close to Jesus and is a reminder that Jesus is always with us.
- Communion is a way we can feel closer to other Christians.

With older children, read together the story of the Last Supper from the Bible and talk about it. Talk with your pastor about Communion if questions arise that you cannot answer or are not sure about.

We are welcomed to God's Table through Communion. God calls parents and other members of the faith community to be the vessels for extending the invitation to our children, and to be facilitators for their continued understanding of this meaningful occasion in their lives and the life of the church.

WHEN WE ATTEND CHURCH WITH OUR CHILDREN,

- we remember in selecting a church to
  - make it a "family affair"
  - pray for God's direction
  - locate churches in our area
  - look for a church to meet the needs of our family, but also look for a church where our family can make a contribution
  - be mindful that a healthy church will have a strong emphasis on outreach
  - not make a hasty decision, but make a decision;
- we make the transition from joining to truly belonging, committing ourselves to consistent church attendance;
- we present our children for baptism;
- we kneel at the Lord's Table together;
- we give of ourselves as well as involving our children in the life of the church, encompassing good stewardship of our time, talents, and money;
- we celebrate special times within the life of the church as a family.

4
WALKING THE VALLEYS WITH OUR CHILDREN

Our daughter, Julie, had just celebrated her fourth birthday and knew that she would soon have her own baby brother or sister. She was eagerly anticipating this joyful event, as was our entire family! One week after Julie's birthday, James Scott Downing was born. Julie finally had a baby brother. She could not have been more excited. She could not wait to see him, hold him, play with him, and "help" Mommy and Daddy take care of him. Julie was a big sister! There was a problem, though. Scottie was born with spina bifida, an opening of the spine. He had this neurological birth defect in its severest form. On Tuesday, April 3, 1979, twenty-nine days after his birth, Scottie died. Time and time again in the midst of our intense grief, we gave thanks to God for our parents, who had had us baptized into the community of faith, where we learned to love and trust God in all the circumstances of life. Over and over my husband and I lifted our thanks to God for the overwhelming love and support our family received from the faith community. We thought of Julie, her sadness, and the deep hurt we were experiencing for her. But underlying it all was the strong renewed affirmation we felt for our decision to have her baptized and exposed to the Christian faith.

At the young age of four Julie was thrust into a valley. Her experience is not unique. All children are faced with many difficult times during their lives. Working together to help instill in our children a faith in God will equip them to survive, to grow through these valleys, and to experience the healing power of God's love.

Lord, we come before you in prayer for our children.

Help us to lovingly reach out, clasp their hands, and draw them ever nearer to you.

Fill us with your love so that we are able to embrace our children during times of sadness, confusion, and doubt.

WHAT ARE THE VALLEYS?

Before we discuss in detail how we can help our children survive these valleys, let us take time to first examine what the valleys are and their causes. Valleys come in all shapes and sizes and know no economic boundaries. No child is immune to them. They tend to fall into some broad identifiable categories.

Separation

When one thinks of this word, words such as *alone, broken, distance, apart, away from, without,* and *divide* come to mind. These words define well the circumstances that plunge children into valleys because of separation. This separation comes under many guises. Children experience separation when their parents get a divorce. Divorce breaks up a whole into parts. It often puts parent against parent, with the child in the middle. Many times the parents are so caught up in their own feelings about the divorce that the child's feelings are ignored.

An offshoot of death or divorce is the blended or step family. These families, which result from remarriages, can bring to the surface such feelings as jealousy, insecurity, fear, and rejection.

Another form of separation is caused by moving, which can be traumatic for a child. I will never forget the job-related move our family made from Knoxville to Nashville, Tennessee. Julie, who was ten years old at the time, was leaving the only home she had ever known, her friends, and the security of the familiar. For many months after our move Julie often cried and begged us to return to Knoxville. How we ached inside for her!

Moving also separates families. My husband often talks of the wonderful memories he has of his childhood. His most wonderful memories are of family times—fishing with his Uncle Richard, gathering for a family reunion in the country. Grandparents, aunts, uncles, cousins were always close by. This family closeness gave Jim a network of love and security. Unfortunately, the majority of families do not have easy access to this kind of network anymore.

Children frequently experience anxiety related to separation when they go to a new school or daycare class. This is true for older children as well as younger children. In any kind of parent-child relationship, good communication is essential; but when children are in the hands of another caregiver for a greater portion of the day, good communication is crucial. Children need the assurance that their parents are there to listen, guide, support, and love them. Without this family interaction, detecting and dealing with our children's needs become increasingly difficult.

Death separates. It indicates finality. Children frequently experience the loss of a grandparent. Often this is the first confrontation children have with the death of someone close to them. Not as common but certainly a possibility during childhood is the loss of a sibling, a close friend, or even a parent. Tragically, in the past five years two fathers of children who attended the day school where I teach have committed suicide. Sadly, too, our society is seeing more and more children as the innocent victims of violent acts. We must recognize that children need to grieve. Children need help to openly express their feelings about death, especially when someone close to them dies. Otherwise the stress can be harmful, both mentally and physically.

During difficult times such as the death of someone close, parents have the tendency to want to shelter their children from the experience. Or they convince themselves that their child is somehow not really attuned to what is happening. Both of these are misconceptions. Children need for us to include them and to help them be a real part of the healing process. When we pray with our children, we are doing just that. We are acknowledging that yes, they are experiencing a valley, and we are working with them toward healing.

Pressure to be the best

The unrealistic pressure on children from parents, teachers, and others to excel in all they do can put children in a valley of discouragement and low self-esteem. While children should be encouraged to do their best at school and extra activities, their best might be labeled average or below average in accordance with "worldly" standards. Adults often

Children need help to openly express their feelings about death, especially when someone close to them dies.

burden children with high and unrealistic expectations and then criticize them when they do not meet these expectations. We also tend to involve our children in so many extracurricular activities that between these and homework, little time is left for family and children just to be themselves. This drive to excel that children feel is coupled with a growing feeling of competition with their peers. It is all right to be competitive to a certain degree, but an excessive amount of competitiveness can hurt relationships, damage self-esteem, and put children under great pressure. One of the best goals we can instill in our children is that of striving to be the best they can be without comparing themselves with everyone else. It is unfortunate that many children today are trying so hard to please everyone else that they fail to develop the unique talents and skills God has given them.

Need for acceptance

Children, just as adults, have a deep need to be accepted and loved by others. When circumstances cause children to feel otherwise, undue stress results and children find themselves "walking in a valley." Unfortunately, in our society today acceptance is too often defined as going along with the crowd, projecting the proper image, and having material things instead of celebrating the uniqueness of each individual. Just as we put designer labels on clothes, we put labels on each other. Negative labels result from teasing, making fun of, judging, naming, singling out, rejecting, and excluding. They prompt children to be somebody they are not, they lower self-esteem, and they often become so permanently ingrained that it takes years to remove them. A child who is constantly told, "You are dumb," soon believes it and loses hope of improving. On the other hand, children who are told over and over again, "You are special. God loves you," learn to feel good about themselves.

The desire to be accepted at any cost can lead our children into all kinds of unhealthy addictions and practices, such as smoking, drinking alcoholic beverages, using other drugs, developing eating disorders, and cheating, to name just a few.

Uncontrollable events

When I was five years old, our house was struck by a tornado. Our roof and back porch were blown off. I still have vivid memories of that night and a real respect for the power of tornadoes. Events such as physical disaster, illness, and all sorts of major or minor accidents occur, and we often have little or no control over them. As much as we would like to protect our children, they are not sheltered from these occurrences. When such events happen, they can place families right in the center of a valley. How parents help their children cope with such events can influence children for the rest of their lives.

In a further attempt to define the valleys, or crises, that can find their way into our children's lives, let me relate to you these staggering statistics from the *State of America's Children Yearbook, 1996* (Washington, DC: Children's Defense Fund):

- Each day, 2,700 babies are born into poverty.
- Each day, 720 babies are born at a low birth weight.
- Each day, 8,640 children are reported abused or neglected.
- Each day, 160 children drop out of school.
- Each day, 360 children are arrested for alcohol-related offenses.
- Each day, 12 children are killed by firearms.

Besides these children who find their way into sociological statistics, there are those from all economic classes in treatment for attention deficit disorder, hyperactivity, obesity, conduct disorder, eating disorder, depression, and addiction.

HOW CAN WE HELP?

So we view the myriad of crises our children can be confronted with. It appears overwhelming. What response do we make? Where do we turn from here? How do we embrace our children during times of sadness, confusion, and doubt? We embrace our children by placing them in God's loving arms through holy baptism, being actively involved in the community of faith, and placing God at the center of our lives. God is the source of hope for us and our children. The

A child who is constantly told, "You are dumb," soon believes it and loses hope of improving. On the other hand, children who are told over and over again, "You are special. God loves you," learn to feel good about themselves.

power of God's love is what can lift our children from their valleys. Only through reaching out to God are we enabled to reach out to our children during the crises in their lives.

Let us now explore in greater detail the process for helping our children face crises with faith. The following steps are suggested to help you do this.

Baptism is a beginning

As I stated earlier, baptism is one of the most loving decisions you can make for your child. Baptism brings your child within the community of faith. It gives a child the Christian nurture and support of the entire faith community. It is the foundation for equipping our children to face the inevitable crises in their lives.

Be part of a church family

Church participation is another foundational step to help our children face crises with faith. When a family is actively involved in a church, it gives that family a network of love and support to which none other can compare. Over and over again in times of trial, I have heard people express, "What would I have done without the church? What would I have done without my faith?" The church is the body of Christ. When we place our children in a church, we bring them into Jesus' loving care. We also place ourselves in his care through the church, which gives us the peaceful assurance that we are not alone when we walk the valleys with our children.

Seek God first

Prayer is a power available to all children no matter who they are, where they are, or what circumstances they are in. Prayer can comfort, ease fear and pain, offer hope, provide a release for feelings, and, most of all, teach our children that God is always with them.

So often in difficult times we pray as a last resort instead of as an initial response. Pray consistently with your child for the Lord's guidance, and encourage your child to tell God specifically what is on his or her mind. Allow children to observe you praying for them and the crisis situation.

As we guide our children in prayer, we must not lead them to think that God automatically gives us what we ask for. We need to emphasize that God loves them and cares for them. Children need help in understanding that God does not will bad things to happen to us, but when bad things do happen, God is always there to care for us and guide us.

Listen to your children and talk with your children

Honest communication is of the utmost importance with our children at any time, but especially during stressful times. Along with encouraging our children to talk through prayer, we need to give the gift of time to our children and encourage them to talk out their feelings with us.

In order for children to talk out their feelings, adults must be good listeners. When we establish this pattern of listening early in our children's lives, we are laying the groundwork for meaningful parent-child communication for a lifetime. If we have not allowed our children to express their hurts, disappointments, concerns, and other feelings before age twelve, we cannot suddenly expect our children to open up to us during the turbulent teenage years, when communication can become strained even under ideal circumstances.

Once we commit ourselves to listen to our children, we can work to help them express what is on their minds. Talking must be defined in its broadest sense here. Children need to be encouraged to let their feelings out in the best way they can for their level of maturity. For some it might be in written form, such as a letter, story, or poem. Younger children can often communicate their feelings more effectively by drawing what they are thinking. Finally, many children will simply use the spoken word to express their thoughts. What is most important is that children's needs not be dismissed by adult inattention.

We must also be forever mindful that when we truly take the time to listen to our children, they often give us the healing words we all need to hear in the midst of a family crisis. The evening our son died we were at home surrounded by family and friends. Julie was there, too. I remember Jim looking

Younger children can often communicate their feelings more effectively by drawing what they are thinking.

at her, tears glistening in his eyes, and saying, "Punkin, Scottie's gone to heaven to be with God. We'll not see him again." "Oh, yes, we will, Daddy," she said. "We'll see him when we get to heaven."

Draw strength and hope from God's Word, the Bible

Scripture is a tremendous source of comfort during troubled times. Children need to know this, and parents need to convey this idea to their children. While certain verses might be difficult for children to comprehend, we can translate the message of these verses into words our children can understand. We can also teach our children that these thoughts come from the Bible. As an adult, there are two verses of Scripture that have helped sustain me through countless difficulties. They are: "We know that all things work together for good for those who love God, who are called according to his purpose" (Romans 8:28), and "No, in all these things we are more than conquerors through him who loved us. For I am convinced that neither death, nor life, nor angels, nor rulers, nor things present, nor things to come, nor powers, nor height, nor depth, nor anything else in all creation, will be able to separate us from the love of God in Christ Jesus our Lord" (Romans 8:37-39).

In talking with your children about these verses, you can impart to them how much God loves us and is always with us, and that because of this love there is always hope. Nothing that we say or do, and nothing that happens to us can cause God to stop loving us. Even the youngest children can realize that God loves and cares for them in a special way, and that we learn this from the Bible. Children can also hear how the Bible tells us that Jesus turned to God in prayer for guidance.

As your children grow older, you can help them understand more fully these teachings from the Bible about God's will during our sad times:

• God does not cause bad things to happen to us.

• When we are hurting, God hurts with us deeply!

- God wants to help us through our sad times. God makes this happen through the love of others for us. When others show love to us, they are loving us for God. When we show love to another, we are helping that person feel God's love.
- Even though we cannot see God, we are never alone. God is always with us.

Encourage children to be active participants

In an attempt to make it easier on our children or shield them in a crisis situation, parents often tend to tell their children what they should do instead of involving the children in the decision-making process. There is a real distinction between telling our children what to do and talking with them in a way that leads them to make their own decisions and goals about handling a crisis. Even young children can be allowed to choose from several good suggestions you give to them in crisis situations. In the case of a physical disaster, illness of a loved one, or other such crisis, children of any age can be given some responsibility that makes them feel like they are contributing. Actively involving our children in the healing process in any way we can is an affirmation of them and gives them renewed confidence and hope.

Practice patience

Unfortunately there is not a quick exit from many of life's valleys. We are unable to confine them to a time frame. They need to be dealt with a bit at a time. It is difficult to be patient when we know that our children are hurting. It is imperative that adults who are trying to help children cope be supportive by keeping communication lines open (with God, too!) and by recognizing any progress made, no matter how little. Adults should always be sensitive to children's setbacks and willing to offer a sympathetic ear when a child experiences them. Comments such as, "You should really be over this by now," can be harmful to a child. Replace such comments with one such as, "I am so proud of the progress you are making!" or, "God knows how hard you are trying." Being lovingly patient with our children not only helps them survive a crisis but teaches them patience with themselves, others, and God.

In the case of a physical disaster, illness of a loved one, or other such crisis, children of any age can be given some responsibility that makes them feel like they are contributing.

Be a loving example for your children

The way parents walk their valleys has a direct effect on how our children confront their crises. When parents consistently reflect an attitude of bitterness, hopelessness, and blaming God for the problems they have, their children are learning to do the same. On the other hand, parents who count their blessings, look for the good in all of life's experiences, and trust that God walks with them through their valleys are giving their children the tools to face life with faith and courage.

Give thanks and praise to God

It is so crucial that we impart to our children the understanding that God does not want bad things to happen to us. God loves us and hurts when we are hurting. To blame God for our trials is a dead end. It results in despair and defeat. What we need to do instead is help our children focus on the good in all the circumstances of life. We can accomplish this in part by guiding our children to recognize how God loves us and helps us survive our valleys through the love of others. For instance, when people respond to the death of a child's grandparent with caring words, hugs, the gift of food, visits, or other expressions of love, say a prayer of thanks to God with your child for these gestures, or simply express to your child, "This is how God shows love to us." During difficult times, acknowledge daily with your children that God does not leave us alone but is here to comfort us. Then identify with them the ways God is touching their lives. When we strive to instill in our children an attitude of thanks and praise to God, we are instilling in them a growing trust in God. We are helping them come to believe that nothing can separate us from the love of God.

Share experiences

The rewards of helping our children rise above their valleys are great. Children gain confidence, develop self-esteem, and become equipped to show God's love to others in similar situations. We can also teach our children how ministering to others is a means of showing our thanks and praise to God. To this day, I feel an immediate bond with families whose infants have died, and have a deep desire to tell them about our experience with Scottie. Likewise, all of us have life crises that give us a ministry to others having some of the same experiences.

Children, too, need to connect with others who have had similar experiences. They need to talk with other children who are working through and surviving crises such as divorce, a move, physical disaster, or the death of a loved one. This interaction benefits our children in many ways. It gives them a unique opportunity to reach out to others. It helps children come to realize that their feelings are, for the most part, normal and that they are not the only ones who have them. And it also helps give children hope and confidence to face the future and a sense of belonging.

As Christian parents we have a responsibility to reach out to all children. Parents and other concerned adults need to help initiate and develop support ministries specifically for our children. Recently our church formed a support group for children of divorced parents. The possibilities for outreach to our children are endless and the blessings many!

As individual families we also need to reach out to other families in distress. A family who has known the devastation of a flood can certainly minister in a meaningful way to other flood victims. Reaching out as a family draws family members closer, unites family members for a common purpose, and gives children a positive message about the value of helping others.

It is so crucial that we impart to our children the understanding that God does not want bad things to happen to us. God loves us and hurts when we are hurting.

Walking the Valleys With Our Children

WHEN WE WALK THROUGH VALLEYS WITH OUR CHILDREN,

- we embrace our children by placing them in God's loving arms through holy baptism;

- we are actively involved in the community of faith;

- we acknowledge that God is the source of our hope and that God's love can help us and our children through the valleys;

- we listen to our children and talk with our children, encouraging them to express their feelings;

- we provide opportunities for our children to make decisions;

- we practice patience and rejoice at small steps toward recovery;

- we provide a loving example for our children;

- we give thanks and praise to God, remembering that it is not God's will that bad things happen and that God will sustain us through hard times.

Conclusion

God has entrusted a precious gift to you. With God's help
and the support of the community of faith you can live out
your calling to parenthood. As you continue to grow in your
discipleship, may this prayer become your prayer:

Lord, we come before you in prayer for our children.
Help us to lovingly reach out, clasp their hands, and draw
    them ever nearer to you.
We lift up our thanks and praise to you for the blessing of
    our children.
We affirm their presence in our lives.
We discover that as we strive to instill within our children a
    growing faith in you, God, a beautiful thing happens:
We become recipients and grow in our faith, also.

We are . . .
Parents and children learning together.
Parents and children guiding one another.
Parents and children sustained by your abundant and
    everlasting love.
Parents and children not only on a journey for ourselves but
    on a journey to help keep your message of love alive for
    all children to come!
Amen. Amen.

Suggested Resources

CHILDREN'S BOOKS

The following books focus on the beauty and wonder of God's world:

God Must Like to Laugh, by Helen Caswell (Nashville: Abingdon Press, 1987).

God's Quiet Things, by Nancy Sweetland (Grand Rapids: William B. Eerdmans Publishing Company, 1994).

Happy Day, by Ruth Krauss (New York: Harpercrest, 1949).

The Very Hungry Caterpillar, by Eric Carle (New York: The Putnam Publishing Group, 1984).

Too Tired, by Ann Turnbull (Orlando: Harcourt Brace & Company, 1994). A delightful telling of Noah's ark.

These books center around what God and Jesus are like:

I Know Who Jesus Is, by Helen Caswell (Nashville: Abingdon Press, 1996).

I Wanted to Know All About God, by Virginia L. Kroll (Grand Rapids: William B. Eerdmans Publishing Company, 1994).

The Runaway Bunny, by Margaret Wise Brown (New York: HarperCollins Children's Books, 1974).

The theme of these books is sharing God's love:

God's Love Is for Sharing, by Helen Caswell (Nashville: Abingdon Press, 1987).

Miss Tizzy, by Libba Moore Gray (New York: Simon & Schuster Children's Publishing Division, 1993).

The Rainbow Fish, by Marcus Pfister (New York: North-South Books, Incorporated, 1992).

Wilfrid Gordon McDonald Partridge, by Mem Fox (Brooklyn: Kane Miller Book Publishers, 1985).

God Speaks to Us in Feeding Stories, by Mary Ann Getty-Sullivan (Collegeville, MN: The Liturgical Press, 1997).

The following are seasonal books:

The Christmas Star, by Marcus Pfister (New York: North-South Books, Incorporated, 1997).

The Christmas Miracle of Jonathan Toomey, by Susan Wojciechowski (Cambridge: Candlewick Press, 1995).

Tale of Three Trees, retold by Angela Elwell Hunt (Elgin, IL: Lion Publishing, 1989). Appropriate for Christmas or Easter.

Why Christmas Trees Aren't Perfect, by Richard H. Schneider (Nashville: Abingdon Press, 1988).

The following books contain prayers for children:

Anytime Prayers, by Madeleine L'Engle (Wheaton, IL: Harold Shaw Publishers, 1994).

Bedtime Hugs for Little Ones, by Debby Boone (Eugene, OR: Harvest House Publishers, Incorporated, 1988).

The following are Bibles or Bible stories:

Loaves & Fishes, by Helen Caswell (Nashville: Abingdon Press, 1993).

The Beginners Bible: Timeless Children's Stories, by Karyn Henley (Portland: Multnomah Press, 1989).

The Toddlers Bible, by V. Gilbert Beers (Colorado Springs: Chariot Victor Publishing, 1992).

Too Tired, by Ann Turnbull (Orlando: Harcourt Brace & Company, 1994). A delightful telling of Noah's ark.

The following are other excellent children's resources:

Pockets magazine (Nashville: The Upper Room).

The Fall of Freddie the Leaf, by Leo Buscaglia (New York: Holt, Rinehart, and Winston, 1982). Helps children deal with death.

The Golden Egg Book, by Margaret Wise Brown (Racine: Western Publishing Company, Incorporated, 1976). Beautiful story about the gift of friendship and how we are never alone.

The following books quote children:

Children's Letters to God: The New Collection, by Stuart Hample and Eric Marshall (New York: Workman Publishing Company, 1991).

Just Build the Ark & the Animals Will Come: Children on Bible Stories, by David Heller (New York: Villard Books, 1994).

Adult Books

The following books give adults insight and support in helping our children grow in their faith:

A Prayer for Children, by Ina Hughs (New York: William Morrow & Company, Incorporated, 1995).

Children and Prayer: A Shared Journey, by Betty Shannon Cloyd (Nashville: Upper Room Books, 1997).

Children Worship! by MaryJane Pierce Norton (Nashville: Discipleship Resources, 1997).

Guide My Feet: Prayers and Meditations on Loving and Working for Children, by Marian Wright Edelman (Boston: Beacon Press, 1995).

Helping Children Feel at Home in Church, by Margie Morris (Nashville: Discipleship Resources, 1997).

Talking to Your Child About God, by David Heller (New York: Berkley Publishing Group, 1994).

Teaching the Bible to Elementary Children, by Dick Murray (Nashville: Discipleship Resources, 1997).

Teaching Young Children: A Guide for Teachers and Leaders, by MaryJane Pierce Norton (Nashville: Discipleship Resources, 1997).

Where Does God Live? Questions and Answers for Parents and Children, by Marc Gellman and Thomas Hartman (New York/Liguori, MO: Triumph/Liguori Publications, 1991).

Homemade Christians, by Nancy Marrocco (Winona, MN: Saint Mary's Press, 1995).

Study Guide

INTRODUCTION

This guide is designed for in-depth group study of the book *Hand in Hand: Growing Spiritually With Our Children*. The following guidelines are given to help you make the best use of this study guide:

- This guide is discussion oriented. The group leader will serve more as a facilitator than as a lecturer.

- Each session guide is designed for approximately an hour-and-a-half time frame, with the entire study to be completed in four sessions. If your meeting times are short—forty-five minutes to an hour—consider dividing the study among eight sessions. The important thing is to adapt the sessions to the amount of time your group has, the number of people in your group, and the needs of your group. There is much opportunity for flexibility within this guide.

- Each session guide is designed to correspond to the chapter with the same title. Participants should read the corresponding chapter before each session if possible.

- Each session guide is divided into three key areas, as follows:
    "Growing Through Prayer" (10–15 minutes). This section includes a suggested opening prayer for your group. It is also a time in which joys and prayer requests from the group may be lifted up.
    "Growing Through Reflection and Discussion" (1 hour). Here you will find discussion questions that are related to the corresponding chapter in the book. Consider dividing the group into smaller groups or having group members talk in pairs and then relate their thoughts on some of the questions to the larger group. It is advisable to have a large newsprint tablet, a chalkboard, or some other medium available to record responses to some of the questions.
    "Growing Through Experience" (15 minutes at the close of your session). This section gives suggestions for family experiences that reinforce the ideas in the corresponding chapter. These activities are to be done between the group sessions. Class time designated for this section should be used to review the activities and to give group members the opportunity to choose the activities they may wish to

do. If your study group meets in a weekend retreat setting or other condensed time frame, recommend that families try the suggested experiences on their own schedule.

- When possible, gather some of the books and other resources suggested in each chapter or in the Suggested Resources list for group members to see or to check out.

- Above all, pray and ask the Lord's guidance as a leader or member of the study group.

My prayer is that God will use this book to help people have a greater understanding of how we can help our children grow in their Christian faith and how we, in turn, can grow in ours.

SESSION 1:
Praying With Our Children

GROWING THROUGH PRAYER

Hold hands with one another as you pray the following:

> Lord, we come before you in prayer for our children.
> Help us to lovingly reach out, clasp their hands, and
>   draw them ever nearer to you.
> Make us aware of the tremendous privilege and
>   responsibility we are entrusted with.
> Help us as, hand in hand, we grow in faith together.
> Amen.

GROWING THROUGH REFLECTION AND DISCUSSION

- What words or thoughts come to mind when you think of prayer? Record these responses.

- Think of one or more prayer experiences you had as a child, or one of the first times you remember praying. Tell the group about these experiences.

- How has prayer influenced your life? Tell about one of the most meaningful prayer experiences you have had if you feel led to.

- How can we lovingly begin to touch our children's lives with prayer? What specific purpose(s) does each of these ways serve?

- Spontaneous moments offer a lot of opportunity for prayer with our children. Envision and discuss what some of these spontaneous moments might be. Tell about one or more spontaneous times of prayer your family has had. What do these times teach our children about prayer?

- What are some opportunities for weaving intentional prayer experiences within your family life? How do our children and our families as a whole benefit from intentional prayer?

- Through what different means can we help our children give expression to their prayers? Tell about any personal examples you have.

- Listening to God is an important component of prayer. How does God speak to us? What are some things we want our children to understand about how God answers prayer?

- Read together the Lord's Prayer from the Bible (Matthew 6:9b-13). Explore it a phrase at a time and talk about what this prayer can teach us. Take time to write this prayer in your own words.

GROWING THROUGH EXPERIENCE

Select one or more of the following activities to do before the next session. Be prepared to tell the group during the next session what you have learned from these experiences.

- Keep a journal of family prayer times. Include time, place, people involved, reason for prayer, and feelings about the experience.

- Write a prayer for your child. Present it to your child, or pray it with him or her.

- Take time to pray the Lord's Prayer with your child and talk with him or her about it.

- Designate a container—a jar, a decorated bag, a vase—for written family prayer requests. Encourage family members to write their requests on individual slips of paper and put them in the container. Once a day or week, read the requests and pray for them as a family.

| SESSION 2:
Reading the Bible With Our Children

GROWING THROUGH PRAYER

Hold hands with one another as you pray the following:

> Lord, we come before you in prayer for our children.
> Help us to lovingly reach out, clasp their hands, and
>   draw them ever nearer to you.
> Make us aware of the tremendous privilege and
>   responsibility we are entrusted with.
> Give us the ability to explore the Bible with our
>   children so that they may come to know you and
>   your will for their lives.
> Instill within us ways to show our children an
>   appreciation for your world.
> Help us as, hand in hand, we grow in faith together.
> Amen.

GROWING THROUGH REFLECTION AND DISCUSSION

- Invite group members to talk about their family prayer experiences since the last session, "Praying With Our Children."

- What thoughts or words come to mind when you think about the Bible? (Record individual responses).

- What recollections of the Bible from your childhood do you have? What influence have your childhood experiences with the Bible had on your life?

- Setting an example is one of the most important means we have of showing our children that the Bible needs to play a vital role in their lives. What are some specific ways we can set an example? Tell how someone's example influenced your use of the Bible.

- What means do parents have of talking with their children about the Bible? How can we introduce children to the Bible?

- How have Bible verses and Bible stories become a real part of your life experience? What are some Bible verses and stories that are significant to you? How does this help us see how we can help our children relate Scripture to their lives?

- God is love, and living our lives in loving response to God's everlasting love for us is central to the teaching of the Bible. We teach our children to live love by giving them the inner assurance that they are loved and by setting a loving example for them. Discuss specific ways this can be accomplished.

- God's world presents us with wonderful opportunities to help our children grow in their love of God and their caring for all of creation. What opportunities does the area you live in offer? Consider the climate, terrain, and environmental needs of your community in your response.

- Read Matthew 18:1-5, part of which reads, "Truly I tell you, unless you change and become like children, you will never enter the kingdom of heaven." Think about your own children or some children you know. What qualities do they possess that show us how God wants us to live the teachings of the Bible? Tell about one or more times when a child has taught you a valuable lesson about life.

GROWING THROUGH EXPERIENCE

Select one or more of the following activities to do before the next session. Be prepared to tell the group during the next session what you have learned from these experiences.

- Read and talk about a Bible story with your child. Then invite your child to tell or illustrate the story for you.

- Commit to setting aside time daily for your personal reading of the Bible.

- Plan a family outing or project centered around an appreciation for God's world, for example a picnic, a hike, or a zoo trip.

- Write a letter to your child expressing God's love and your love for him or her. Include gifts and qualities you feel that your child possesses.

| Study Guide | SESSION 3:
Attending Church With Our Children |

SESSION 3:
Attending Church With Our Children

GROWING THROUGH PRAYER

Hold hands with one another as you pray the following:
> Lord, we come before you in prayer for our children.
> Help us to lovingly reach out, clasp their hands, and
> draw them ever nearer to you.
> Make us aware of the tremendous privilege and
> responsibility we are entrusted with.
> Awaken in us the need to become an active part of
> the community of faith.
> Impress on our hearts the importance of celebrating
> and sharing special times together in the life of
> the church.
> Help us as, hand in hand, we grow in faith together.
> Amen.

GROWING THROUGH REFLECTION AND DISCUSSION

- Invite group members to discuss their family Bible-related experiences since the last session, "Reading the Bible With Our Children."

- As a group, complete the phrase, "The church is . . . " (Record the responses.)

- What meaning does the church have for you now? What role did it play in your childhood?

- How did you select your present church or other churches you have belonged to? In your estimation, what criteria are most important?

- What is the distinction between attending and belonging to a church? What opportunities are there for involvement at your church?

- What makes baptism such a significant part of one's spiritual growth? How can we make our children aware of the profound meaning of this sacrament in their lives?

- What images come to mind when you think of the sacrament of Communion? What feelings surface? What thoughts about Communion can we explore with our children to give them a better understanding of it?

- How can we help our families go from hectic to holy during the Advent and Christmas seasons? What Advent and Christmas traditions has your family established to help you do this? Which church programs are the most meaningful for your family?
- In what ways can families focus on the message of love and joy God gives us at Easter?

GROWING THROUGH EXPERIENCE

Select one or more of the following activities to do before the next session. Be prepared to tell the group during the next session what you have learned from these experiences.

- Commit as a family to perform some act of kindness for another person, family, or group each day or as many days as possible.
- Pray with your child and ask God if there is a specific need your family can fulfill for the church, or any new ways you can be involved.
- Write a note of thanks to your child's Sunday school teacher or another staff person at your church to express your family's appreciation for his or her dedication to the church.
- Invite another person or family to attend church with you.

SESSION 4:
Walking the Valleys With Our Children

GROWING THROUGH PRAYER

Hold hands with one another as you pray the following:

Lord, we come before you in prayer for our children.
Help us to lovingly reach out, clasp their hands, and
draw them ever nearer to you.
Make us aware of the tremendous privilege and
responsibility we are entrusted with.
Fill us with your love so that we are able to embrace
our children during times of sadness, confusion,
and doubt.
Help us as, hand in hand, we grow in faith together.
Amen.

Study Guide

- Invite group members to discuss their family church-related experiences since the previous session, "Attending Church With Our Children."

- Identify crises you have experienced. (Record these responses.) Identify feelings that surfaced during these times. (Make note of these separately.)

- Discuss the primary factors that helped you survive and grow from the crises.

- What are some of the "valleys" our children are faced with today?

- What kind of attitude toward God and crisis do we hope to instill in our children?

- What is God's will during these difficult times? What choices do our children have?

- Review the steps suggested on pages 78–83 in Chapter 4 for helping our children face their crises with faith. Discuss as a group how each step contributes to the healing process.

- In what ways is your church a source of support for children faced with crisis situations? How could this support be improved? What could your class, group, or you as an individual do about it?

GROWING THROUGH EXPERIENCE

It is hoped that the completion of this study has prompted many new beginnings as we attempt to instill within our children the foundation for a growing Christian faith. With love for our children, the following activity suggestions are offered for your consideration:

- Commit to daily prayer for your children and the children of the world.

- Form a parent support group from members of this study. Plan to meet on a regular basis to pray for children and to explore ways to touch them with God's love.

- Ask God to show you how you can be in ministry to children.

- Through your church or a local agency, "adopt" a child or family to love and give support to in exceptional ways.